Michael
Wow! What An
Amazing Journey.
Thank you for
All your faith &
Support.
Let's Climb!

PEAK PERFORMANCE

PEAK
PERFORMANCE

THE FIVE PRINCIPLES
EVERY GREAT BUSINESS LIVES BY

GREGORY CLEARY

PEAK PERFORMANCE
The Five Principles Every Great Business Lives By
ISBNs: 979-8-218-65771-0 (hc); 979-8-218-69314-5 (pbk);
979-8-218-69315-2 (ebk)

CONTENTS

REACH YOUR PINNACLE

Do you want to be a "category-of-one" company, so successful, you define the space, your name synonymous with what you do, like Uber or Google?

Pinnacle Business Guides® can get you up that mountain.

Whether your goal is to grow 20 percent next year, open three new locations, expand into a new service line, or dominate an entire industry, Pinnacle Business Guides exists to help you define your top goal — your personal Pinnacle — uncover the path up the mountain and focus your team on getting there.

Business operating systems — prepackaged frameworks that helps organizations improve operations with various tools and methods — have become popular in recent years. They can improve operations and efficiency, helping businesses to run like self-sustaining machines. Pinnacle has expanded on this model. While we also bring operational efficiency, we've added a focus on strategy that allows you to reach an audacious goal, the Pinnacle of your particular mountain.

Having worked with other operating systems, I wanted to create a new approach with Pinnacle, one built around expert Guides for businesses — people with deep experience, flexibility, and a bigger array of tools, which would be tailored to each company's needs.

Most important, these Guides would meet clients where they were, adjusting to fit their needs and evolving alongside their businesses.

Most business operating systems offer **prescriptions**. They take a one-size-fits-all approach, which means they don't fit anyone. Pinnacle Business Guides replaced that model with a **principle-based approach**. We have distilled success and organizational health into five fundamental principles, or in a sense, four that inevitably lead to a fifth:

PEOPLE + PURPOSE + PLAYBOOKS

This is the winning formula. We help leadership teams address everything from core values and culture to meetings that matter and true accountability through the lens of these five key principles. Together, they cover every part of your business, and we have an enormous toolbox to assess, support, and improve team efforts in each of these key areas. Our tools are carefully curated — time-tested solutions and concepts created or drawn from various sources for maximum efficacy. They can be customized to fit your business, and if we don't have the right tool to meet a need, we'll find it or build it.

No one has cornered the market on good ideas (just check the variety of apps on your phone), so a focus on flexible Guides and principles rather than set prescriptions allows us to pick and choose the very best from all over. The result is a customized operating system that fits your business like a finely tailored suit, not a prepackaged structure you wear like a blazer off the rack. No two businesses are the same, so we believe that no two business operating systems should be exactly the same.

Pinnacle Business Guides' approach has been decades in the making. My own journey started in 1985, selling and teaching the curriculum of Brian Tracy, author of *The Psychology of Selling* and creator of The Phoenix Seminar. Tracy's program focused on self-improvement, goal achievement, communication, relationships, and health. I went on to become the National Sales Manager for the Peak Performers Network, the Co-Founder of Team Trac, and the Founder of Action Learning Corporation.

+ PERFORMANCE = PROFITS

My experience in business, sales, and coaching led me to the Entrepreneurial Operating System in 2010, when I became the eighth certified implementor in the world. Soon, I was the first implementor to earn more than $1 million in annual fees and over a decade, I worked with 149 companies, running more than 1,000 documented sessions. I was the implementor teaching the implementors, to put the experience in perspective, in a class called Sales Mastery, and I was the number one implementor in terms of both sessions conducted and revenue when I departed in 2019.

I knew there was a better way. I felt like I'd been training and studying all my life to develop and deliver value to ambitious entrepreneurs in search of a path up the mountain. I co-founded Pinnacle in 2020 with Duane Marshall, and despite tough timing — COVID was also getting underway — we grew quickly. We hoped to have 20 Guides that year — an ambitious goal, considering. By year-end, we had 60. As I write this, we're at 130, and by the end of 2025, we'll have 200 Guides — experienced professional business coaches, CEO peer group leaders, and former CEOs and business owners who have made the climb themselves. I handpick every Guide, and we could have grown even faster if our standards weren't so high.

I wrote my first book to introduce our Guides and five principles to entrepreneurs in 2022. So much has changed, though, and we've grown so quickly, I felt that it was already time for a better book. I decided to write a completely new book with fresh examples and a tighter narrative that would be easier to follow, keeping not a single page from the old book.

Chapter 1 is an introduction to Pinnacle, with an overview of our model and Guides, as well as the five principles, exploring the service that makes us different. I then spend a chapter on each of the five fundamental principles, exploring why it's vital for your growth and organizational health. I'll share practical methods, stories from the trenches, and a taste of our tools to illustrate how you can build strategy and improve operations in each area. I hope you'll come away from this book with new ideas for achieving ambitious goals and optimizing the machine of your business. The idea is to have it running so smoothly, leaders can focus on leading and ultimately, reaching their Pinnacle.

The most salient number I can provide as you start that journey isn't how many Guides we have or other metrics of our growth, it's 21 percent — that's the average annual growth rate Pinnacle Business Guides clients have experienced, though we have many examples of clients seeing growth of 100 percent, 300 percent, or more. The businesses that we help range from small family-owned companies with one location to national brands with billions in assets.

They all have one thing in common. They want the machine of their business to hum effortlessly, so that they can focus on growth. They have their eyes on the Pinnacle, and our Guides are determined to get them to the top. In this book, you will find practical, tested solutions to the core problems you face in building your business. We sincerely hope this helps you grow and make an impact in your community.

Let's Climb!™

— Gregory Cleary
Naples, Florida, March FORTH(!), 2025

CHAPTER 1

THE PINNACLE
DIFFERENCE

Hempel Real Estate was an extremely successful commercial real estate and development firm in Minneapolis when I began working with them as a Pinnacle Business Guide, but like most good companies, they wanted to be a great company.

CEO Josh Krsnak is a classic visionary with a 24-year tenure at Hempel. He started as the first employee, eventually bought the firm from its founder, Jon Hempel, and proceeded to oversee the purchase and development of more than $1 billion in commercial real estate — properties like the Minneapolis Loews Hotel (now The Lofton), the Shops at West End, and LaSalle Plaza, a 30-story office tower in the heart of downtown. Hempel picked up LaSalle, a modern limestone and glass skyscraper with an Art Deco feel, then added a new lobby, lighting, pickleball courts, a roof deck, you name it, boosting its value and attraction for tenants.

Hempel's portfolio is full of similar success stories, but Josh told me that he wanted more growth. I knew within our first five minutes that this was a visionary who would not be satisfied with anything lower than the top of the mountain. In that pursuit, Hempel had spent several years working with a popular business operating system before I came on board.

As many readers know, a business operating system, or OS, is an outside framework that helps organizations improve operations with a set of tools and methods. The idea is to systemize things, find a rhythm for the business, and boost productivity with more effective meetings, measures, planning, and accountability. Every business has an OS, whether they realize it or not. Just as every business has an operating system, so does every marriage, school, sports team — any entity that engages in an activity more than once. Unfortunately, organic systems developed on an ad-hoc basis are often half-invisible and imperfectly understood, even by their creators.

The formalized OS argument is that a more conscious and efficient system with better tools saves leaders time, so they can work *on* the business — thinking about the big picture — and not just *in* the business — consumed by daily headaches. Some companies install an OS on their own, and others get help from a coach, as Hempel did.

FINDING THE PATH

During day one of our "Base Camp," which is the initial meeting Pinnacle Business Guides have with leadership teams to envision a bolder future, Hempel leaders described the kind of serious growth they were after. We think of this kind of target as a company's particular "Pinnacle," or number one goal. I kept it front and center as a lively conversation ensued, although uncomfortable at times. After discussing the desired growth with the leadership team, I dove straight into The Brutal Facts©, an exercise we adapted from Jim Collins' *Good to Great: Why Some Companies Make the Leap...And Others Don't*, to lay out what was keeping them from that goal.

Feathers frequently get ruffled in these conversations, but like most natural leaders who engage in them, Josh welcomed the discomfort.

> "Do you know the difference between you and our last coach?"

Josh said when we broke for lunch. "It occurred to me this morning as we talked. All our former coach did was try to please me and keep the gig alive. You have no interest in pleasing me or following an agenda. We said we want to grow, and you're pushing us to grow, and after four hours, we're already thinking differently."

We believe that one of the most important things we do as Pinnacle Business Guides is to help leadership teams improve their thought process and ultimately, gain more clarity in their thinking.

As we planned for Hempel's growth over a number of sessions, I watched the company's pros at work and noticed a pattern. Hempel would find a desirable property and have to raise $5 million to acquire it. They would contact their investors that morning — they had about 1,000 at the time — and by 4 p.m., they would have raised $10 million. These pros were good at raising capital, so good that the deal was overfunded. A nice problem to have in a way, but not the most efficient system. This topic came up in our session. The leaders in the room agreed there must be a better way, though at first, not about what that should be.

We debated the optimal path and after discussion, landed on the idea that the company should create a fund. If Hempel had $20 million or $30 million on hand to invest, the firm could pounce on deals faster — no scrambling to raise money and no over-funding. Investors know the company's sterling track record, so raising that sizeable amount was feasible — and better for investors, who would see their risk spread over multiple projects.

We incorporated this ambitious target into our Strategic Vision & Execution Plan© (a Pinnacle tool customized for Hempel), along with goals to help us get to the Pinnacle, mid-term mile-stones to mark progress, Rocks (the smaller goals that get us to the bigger ones), and other elements that made creating this fund a cornerstone of the Annual Growth Plan. From that Strategic Vision, we worked backwards to lay out the detailed strategies, personnel changes, and other measures that would get us up the mountain (three leadership team departures and three new members, for instance, including an A-player from a huge competitor).

As I write this, Hempel just finished an incredible year of growth, with 45 commercial properties purchased in just 12 months. The company is on its way to raising $40 million for not one, but two funds, and it has launched a "Back 2 Basics" overhaul that's dramatically streamlining and systemizing operations with the help of their Guide and our enormous curated toolbox. The Pinnacle — that elusive growth goal — has moved closer. The new systems in place — streamlined, documented, repeat-able, and scalable — are allowing leaders to spend less time on internal operations and more time on external strategies, keeping their focus on that climb to the top of their mountain.

THE STATIC
OPERATING SYSTEM

I take zero direct credit for Hempel's wildly ambitious goal or for the creative strategies and innovations getting the company to its Pinnacle. The skill, vision, and expertise — in fact, all the answers — were always in that conference room where I huddled with leaders. The optimal path was always there, just as it's always buried somewhere on even the most challenging mountains. The job of a good Guide is simply to provide the best possible climbing tools, direct attention to that path, and facilitate the ascent by extracting those answers and wisdom from the group.

Being a good Guide, though, does require deep experience and a particular skillset. One of those skills, in my opinion, is the ability to recognize an urgent need or problem and pivot to address it, helping to find creative solutions and the perfect tools for a particular climb. (This belief rests on the idea that every problem is also an opportunity, as Hempel amply demonstrates.)

It might seem like common sense, diving into the company's highest priority or biggest shortfall at any given moment to correct course, but the turnkey systems that have become popular in recent years begin where they want to begin, with their built-in priorities, not the client's. The starting place never varies — a fixed point addressed with standard prescriptions and a limited set of static tools.

The problem with these off-the-shelf systems — and one of the reasons I founded Pinnacle — is that they impose prepackaged structures on organizations, without the flexibility to deal with a company's particular needs. This is the prescriptive approach: take this medicine four times daily with food and a full glass of water. If you miss a dose, take your next one right away.

The principle-based approach takes a look at your age, weight, BMI, blood pressure, and other pertinent measurements, then recommends an overall health regimen based on where you're at and where you want to be: Get eight hours sleep every night, walk one mile a day, eat more leafy greens, and cut your alcohol consumption in half. We evolve with you as your health improves, customizing the program. After a year, maybe you need to walk or run two miles a day, hit the gym weekly, and cut the fat, since cholesterol is now borderline. Running a marathon, which seemed like a pipedream, now looks possible, so let's talk about the gradual ascent that will get you to that Pinnacle. We all want to evolve or we get bored — and flabby — and results diminish.

A good operating system can improve operational clarity, as I know from firsthand experience. As I mentioned in the intro-duction, I worked with one for years and rose to its top ranks. We helped lots of businesses, but I always knew that something was missing. The solutions were too rigid and prescriptive. The tools and process never changed, and maybe most important, we didn't meet clients where they were. Instead, we dragged them, sometimes inches and sometimes miles, to the place we wanted them to be.

After decades of experience in sales and marketing with a variety of businesses (more on my checkered career shortly), I understood that every organization has its own culture, goals, and gaps. My practice, which I referred to as "client-centric," reflected this conviction, pulling in lots of outside ideas and tools to fill holes and address specific client needs that our limited tools didn't. I decided to add those things on my own, but it was tough — the system wasn't built for that kind of flexibility. How might it be? I asked myself, how could an operating system be designed to work with clients on their terms, with a wider range of tools that would be flexible, not rigid, and solutions that would be tailored to a company's needs at any given moment?

And then I realized this was the wrong question.

A NEW APPROACH

The world did not need another operating system — there were plenty. It needed a whole new approach. The challenge that perpetually stuck in my head wasn't about building a better system but a continuously better system, one that would always evolve, as flexible and innovative as we told leaders they had to be in today's markets.

Actually, "system" wasn't right either. We needed continuously better "systems," as many as there were businesses. No two companies are exactly alike, so why should an operating system not vary from one to the next? Of course, there would still be tools, in fact, a much wider variety of them, chosen for their relevance and tailored for a perfect fit. But a flexible, evolving system customized for each business and its needs, I quickly understood, would have to be based on principles, not prescriptions.

Which principles? It didn't take me long to distill success down to five vital ones, or really, four principles that inevitably lead to a fifth: People, Purpose, Playbooks, and Performance. Excel in those first four areas, and you're all but certain to enjoy the fifth — Profits (we'll explore all five soon).

The difficulty of a principle-based approach is that it requires much more nuance, understanding, and experience. Anyone can apply a Band-Aid to a scratch, but surgery demands a highly skilled professional. For the kind of service I imagined, we would need highly skilled professionals, the best of the best. They would not be repeating the same routine in a hundred conference rooms each year, but crafting a unique approach for each company based on its needs and five bedrock principles. They would need to master a much larger and more flexible set of tools and be able to pull in more when necessary. Evolution means getting comfortable with discomfort, and these pros would have to be comfortable in a continuously changing system (in case that sounds like hot air, consider the fact that I decided to write a new book because we have evolved so much in three years.)

This was the biggest missing piece of the operating system puzzle, I came to realize, the experts who could unlock an organization's full potential, who could read your business, people who could tailor tools and solutions to your needs, who could evolve alongside a client's business. When a leader like Josh Krsnak, of Hempel Real Estate, tells a Guide that he's addressing the firm's priorities, pushing it to grow, and in a matter of hours, changing leaders' thinking, it validates the origins of Pinnacle Business Guides: a belief that it's all about the right person, not a particular tool or operating system.

When Pinnacle was still just a gleam in my eye, I started thinking of such experts as "Guides," a label that still seems perfect to me. The path to success, as I said, has always been there. Good leaders know this in their bones. An expert Guide helps you to see it. A great Guide knows the terrain and your potential and how to maximize both. The word "Guide" implies expertise, trust, comfort, and confidence. And that title jibed with what has always seemed to me the perfect metaphor for growing a business — mountain climbing. Running a small business is like hiking — you don't need much: A friend, a water bottle, decent shoes, and shorts will do. As you get ambitious, climbing mountains, you need more and better tools, a bigger and better team, real expertise.

The same holds true for a business as it adds employees, runs a bigger payroll, merges, or expands into new areas. Everything gets more complicated, decisions are weightier, the stress and threats grow, and yet, ambition drives on those compelled to excel. Whatever summit they're at, they can't help eyeing higher peaks. They want to get to the Pinnacle, the highest spot on the mountain, and deep down, they know they can do it with a strategic vision, solid tools, and a great Guide.

This is the gap that I founded Pinnacle to fill. How did we get here? I'll back up for just a moment to relate a little of our origin story before exploring more of the Pinnacle model and how the rest of this book is organized to help you.

BORN FOR BUSINESS

I was born in St. John's, in Newfoundland, on Canada's rugged, scenic East Coast. It was a beautiful place but small, cold, and in the 1970s, economically depressed. I don't know if it was genetics or watching my dad hustle, but I'd become a natural businessman in that tough environment by the time I turned 12. I was so driven in my first job, as a paperboy, I took over other kids' routes. At 14, I went from busboy at the famous Skylon Tower in Niagara Falls to captain waiter, and soon after, started my own business, Picnic in the Park. I realized that in the beautiful nearby park in the honeymoon capital of the world, you couldn't buy so much as an ice cream cone. Seeing an opening, I assembled picnic baskets and donned a black tie to deliver them to the lovebirds canoodling there. I made good money and from that moment, was on the lookout for business opportunities.

After school, I went to work for personal development guru Brian Tracy, author of The Psychology of Selling, promoting and selling his sales training class. I didn't make enough to cover my car payment that first month, but I eventually became one of the top salespeople in all of Ontario. At that point, some friends and I moved to Toronto, where we got an apartment in a new building called The Summit.

The company then sent me to Cleveland, where I cold-called any and every business that had a sales team. To drum up interest, I would do free workshops ahead of Tracy's live events, a strategy that put me among the top salespeople and really launched my career. I parlayed that success into a job as national sales manager of the Peak Performers Network and moved to Minneapolis, MN under the mistaken impression that it was well south of Toronto.

At Peak, we packaged top speakers — Tommy Hopkins, Floyd Wickman, Tony Robbins, Brian Tracy, etc. — and sold an annual pass to hear them. I hired all the salespeople, wrote the presentations, and learned everything, top to bottom (after waiting tables in Skylon Tower, living in The Summit, working for Peak Performers, and holding client sessions at a place called The Lodge, at Eagle Creek, in Savage, MN, it feels like destiny that the dots finally connected within Pinnacle Business Guides).

I wanted to get off the road for obvious reasons after September 11, 2001, so I hung out my shingle as a sales coach. I took a different approach, working intimately with businesses to figure out and develop their sales process. I'd have the company create a business card for me, so I could ride with their salespeople to prove that the changes we made worked. The clients loved it, and I had a blast.

In 2010, I met Gino Wickman, whose dad, it turned out, was Floyd Wickman, one of our Peak Performers Network speakers from years earlier. I decided to join Gino, becoming the eighth certified implementor of his new endeavor, the Entrepreneurial Operating System, or EOS. During my decade with EOS, I worked with 149 companies, ran more than 1,000 sessions, and taught a class called Sales Mastery to other implementors. By my departure in 2019, I was number one in both sales and sessions conducted.

I had stayed the course for decades, showing up daily, putting in the proverbial 10,000 hours, building mastery, and staying true to the craft. I decided to go for it and begin my own climb, starting Pinnacle with Duane Marshall, another top business coach. We chose March 4th — the only date of the year that's also a command (March Forth!) — to launch our business. Unfortunately, the year was 2020, and a bomb called COVID was about to detonate. Businesses everywhere faced a new existential threat.

THE PINNACLE MODEL

Okay, it was not the most auspicious time to launch a business, March of 2020, but it would certainly test our mettle. If we can survive this, we thought, we'll survive anything, and more important, we can help lots of other hardworking entrepreneurs, their businesses, and their team members survive too. Maybe it was the worst timing ever, or maybe it was perfect in a strange way, since our services were more necessary than ever.

As the pandemic struck, we immediately went virtual and paused whatever agendas we'd established with leadership teams to do this exercise: I had everyone list the things we could not control — government mandates, people's fears, the virus, duration of the pandemic, etc. — and the things we could. Once we'd made our lists, I asked, how do you want to spend our quarterly Summit today, talking about the things we can control or the things we can't? The answer was obvious, and the exercise got us back on track.

I could write a separate book about how we helped companies through COVID, but just to give one example, a client of mine, Discover Strength, was shut down, like all gyms at the time.

Instead of shuttering their doors, though, when I met with the leadership team for their Quarterly Summit, we agreed that the following morning, we would be a virtual training company. Doesn't matter if the available equipment is weights, chairs, or rubber bands, our clients need us. We're going to keep them healthy through a stressful time, whether that's with squats, pushups, or whatever. The big brands and giant gyms shut down, but my scrappy client, this small fitness studio, flipped to become a virtual company and kept serving their clients.

The pandemic was an exceptional time, but the kind of service we provided then was typical of what I'd always done for clients. My business customers stayed with me forever, partly because I focused so heavily on client experience. I always brought in new tools and concepts, practicing, as I've mentioned, a client-centric approach. I had an enormous toolbox, and I remained a student, eager to read the latest piece on remote work, social media promotions, or AI — a curiosity and passion my clients appreciated.

Pinnacle's momentum despite COVID reflected that focus on client experience but also a shift in the marketplace. I'd watched the evolution while working with hundreds of leadership teams. There was a boom in business books and educational options. Clients kept reading and learning, joining peer groups, and going to Vistage conferences. Fees charged by the business operating systems were going up, and CEOs wanted more value for their buck. Top leaders understood the landscape. They were asking for more and better tools, more help. They wanted true guidance, and Pinnacle Business Guides were perfectly positioned to provide it.

We planned to get to 20 Guides during our first year — an ambitious goal during COVID. Instead, we got to 60. As I write this in early 2025, we're at 130 Guides, as I mentioned in the introduction, and by the end of the year, we'll have 200.

That rapid growth has to do with the Pinnacle difference I touched on earlier. Yes, we excel at getting businesses to operational clarity. We have the know-how and tools to make communications clearer and meetings more effective. We help businesses to improve structure, clearly define roles, and automate processes in order to become truly systems-based. Optimizing the internal machine of the business in this way frees up time for leaders to focus on obstacles and growth.

Such operational clarity is the point at which the best of the operating systems stop. For Pinnacle Business Guides, it's a baseline, the point where the magic begins. I often tell prospective clients to think of their craziest, most ambitious business goal, the kind of dream so lofty, you're reluctant to say it out loud. That's the place where Pinnacle Business Guides shine. We help to define that grand goal, your personal "Pinnacle," and how it makes you different, then work backwards, inventing the strategies and smaller goals that will help us scale the mountain to reach it.

The process starts at a two to three-day intensive Base Camp session where leaders begin to envision a bolder future. We define what your personal Pinnacle is at Base Camp, what the path to it looks like, and which climbing tools might help. We cover big-picture elements such as Purpose and core values, as well as the nitty-gritty ones like meeting structures and 30-day Rocks.

Base Camp is followed up with Quarterly Summits where the members of the leadership team get together for a full day with their guide to "Look Back" and measure progress, "Look Out" to plan for the next Quarter, and "Look Up" to think bigger. We measure and build team health, discuss progress, and adopt new climbing tools as needed. The Annual Overnight Summit covers a lot of ground, with a focus on what's working and what isn't, what strategies are proving effective and how we can address the ones that aren't.

We eat and breathe strategy, which Pinnacle Business Guides see as an integral part of a company's Purpose, an approach I'll explore at length later.

THINK GUIDE, NOT OPERATING SYSTEM

We love building strategy in service of a bold vision because we have Guides who can do it. They spend an enormous amount of time upfront questioning the visionary at a company's helm and their leadership team. What's working? What isn't? What stands in the way of the growth they want to achieve? How would we define success two years from now, looking back over this journey? We listen intently to the answers, considering where leaders want to go and examining the obstacles in their path. We even ask them to name the most likely reasons for failure if two years from now, this process isn't working, so that we can avoid those crevasses.

The key to this journey is having the right Guide asking the right questions and following up on the answers. A great Guide can tailor everything to your business and pull in whatever tools or methods are needed, so the system becomes yours, customized as you get your business up the mountain. It's the best of both worlds — structure and a philosophy that calls for providing the right tool at the right time.

The clients I have had for years now understand the primacy of the Guide better than anyone. They didn't blink when I left to start Pinnacle, in fact, they all followed me. The leaders I work with don't care where I've run sessions or with whom. They care about my expertise and ability to get them up that mountain. Their question is not "what's in your backpack?" but "Can you help me?"

This is why only a small percentage of those who try to become Pinnacle Guides are accepted. "Who first" (meaning People are everything) is a motto we extol to leadership teams, and it's a belief we live by at home. I personally handpick every Guide, pulling most from just three places:

- **PROFESSIONAL COACHES.** The best professional coaches understand leadership teams and how to provide maximum impact.

- **PEER GROUP LEADERS.** Those who have run peer groups through Vistage, Convene, or MacKay CEO Forums are used to working with 50 or 60 entrepreneurs at a time. They know leaders' concerns and speak the entrepreneur's language.

- **CEOs.** People who ran their own successful companies and subsequently sold them understand the value of a good business operating system and how to enlist strategy to reach the Pinnacle because they've done it. They know how to achieve growth through change and have internalized Peter Drucker's adage that "what got you here is not going to get you there."

As I've said, a good Guide helps reveal an existing path to the Pinnacle and focus leaders on its contours. The expertise and strategy — all the answers, in fact — are already in the room, just as the various parts of the business machine are sitting there, waiting to be optimized. A Guide finds the footprints and helps you see the buried path. As media critic Marshall McLuhan wrote, "We don't know who discovered water, but we know it wasn't the fish." Leadership teams are swimming in their own systems, which makes the full array of People and processes impossible to see clearly. A Pinnacle Business Guide helps you rise above the water to analyze and optimize the ecosystem below.

Our Guides have access to a wide variety, and more flexible, tools — 85-plus and counting, as I write this. We customize those tools for our clients, as I've mentioned, and if we don't have the right one, we'll find or build it. Our goal is to assemble the GOAT toolbox. That stands for Greatest Of All Time — and it's no accident that goats are great climbers.

PINNACLE GOAT

Our wider array of flexible tools is one of the big differences between a flexible, principle-based approach and the standard prescriptive approach. If your only tool is a hammer, everything's a nail to be pounded. That's prescription. Guided by principles, we instead say, oh, you're building a ship? Screws will work best for that — let's find you the perfect ones. Rather than people slinging hammers, we are like master mechanics with a Snap-on toolbox 8 feet high and 20 feet long. When you say, we need to start up a client advisory board, we reach into the toolbox and hand you the best practices for client advisory boards. When it's time for you to exit the company, our CEPA-certified Guide, who's an expert in this area, produces a whole set of tools for that transition. Merging and need to create departmental visions that sync up? We reach in and grab the tools that will structure that process without any gaps.

THE PRINCIPLE-BASED APPROACH

Our tools, Guides, Summits, and everything else we do rest on the five key principles that are the foundation of any business: People, Purpose, Playbooks, Performance, and Profits. They cover everything you need for operational success, organizational health, and the kind of growth that takes you to the Pinnacle. The rest of this book is organized around these fundamental principles. I'll spend a chapter on each, discussing how it contributes to process, strategy, and vision, how it can be defined and measured, and how it works with the other four principles. There isn't space to explore all of our tools here, but in each chapter, I'll also give a preview of the tools that Pinnacle Business Guides bring to the table to address these vital principles.

Here's a quick overview of our five principles and a roadmap for the rest of this book:

PEOPLE. It's no accident that People is principle number one (A-players are free is a constant refrain for Pinnacle Guides). Surrounding yourself with the right People is a necessity. You won't get far up that mountain without a crack team. We agree with Jim Collins, who wrote in *Good to Great* that terrific leaders don't start with creating a vision, but with getting the right people in the right seats. You actually need the right people with the right boots and the right tools in the right seats, as I'll explain in Chapter 2. I'll also show how tools like our Talent Assessment©, Level Up©, and The A-Players Draft© are invaluable in this effort.

PURPOSE. For so many, "purpose" has become a squishy, meaningless platitude, something to carve into a plaque then forget. For Pinnacle Business Guides, Purpose is all meat. It is the reason you exist but also encapsulates your Pinnacle (top goal), as well as the vision and strategy that get you up the mountain. Purpose truly builds culture, as I'll explore in Chapter 3, when it's attached not just to noble ideals but also to the stuff we roll up our sleeves to work on each day. I'll introduce our Strategic Vision & Execution Plan, as well as Core Purpose© and Pinnacle worksheets.

PLAYBOOKS. Are you playing to win or not to lose? Playbooks help you play to win by clarifying the structure, processes, roles, and systems that comprise the machine of your business. Optimizing that machine with clear Playbooks is vital if you want to get from the foothills to ever higher peaks. I'll explain how a Guide introduces Playbooks for marketing, sales, projects, accounting, etc. until all the gears are greased and turning on their own, freeing up leaders' time to lead.

PERFORMANCE. Vision and strategy are useless without action. If getting it done were as easy as deciding on strategy and goals, most companies would live at the Pinnacle. Here, I'll introduce some of our most immediately useful tools and ideas, including our Win the Week Scoreboard©, for accountability, and FAST Rocks. Bill Gates, who is reputed to have said that most people overestimate what they can do in one year and underestimate what they can do in 10 years had it right. Achieving peak performance means rebalancing these estimates.

PROFITS. Excel in the first four principles, and you'll enjoy the fifth, Profits. A smart overall strategy gains momentum, growing continually better, faster, and cheaper. With the right People, clear Purpose, detailed Playbooks, and consistent Performance, Profits are nearly inevitable. Gamechangers here include our tools Profit Per X©, Profit First©, and The Impact of One©, which empowers every team member, from the frontline to the corner office, to build Profits.

As outlined in our final principle, the fundamental Pinnacle formula is:

PEOPLE + PURPOSE + PLAYBOOKS + PERFORMANCE = PROFITS

In the coming pages, I'll explain how this formula has worked for countless clients of Pinnacle Business Guides, firms like Hempel Real Estate, which I described at the start of this chapter — the company that bought 45 commercial properties in 2024 and set a goal of raising $30 million for two new funds in 2025 on a journey to its Pinnacle. Some other examples include:

- A Minnesota HVAC business facing down two new competitors, Hero and Blue Ox, with a company-wide effort to "send Hero out of town on a Blue Ox." The campaign is fun, but it's also firing up team members, from technicians to executives, and building competitive advantage as they climb.

- A Pella distributorship has determined after a deep dive into People, Purpose, Playbooks, and Performance with its Pinnacle Guide, that a new focus on customer experience will boost the service it offers — and, of course, Profits. Leaders have realized that delivering an exceptional customer experience must start with delivering an exceptional experience for team members.

- Union Bank and Trust, one of the only union-owned banks in the U.S., is embarking on a campaign to add $1.5 B in assets under management this year and a plan to provide highly profitable financial services to the cannabis industry — and is seeing its first significant growth in a very long time.

- Gardener Builders, a client of several years, has grown into a $400 million company, evolving to the point that it can focus a People initiative on the emerging leaders who will carry on the climb with continued growth.

It's a rare company that sits on the side of the mountain perfectly balanced, neither rising nor falling. If you're not climbing, you're likely falling, whether you know it or not. We understand this well at Pinnacle Business Guides, where our money and mouth are always in the same vicinity. Our own Pinnacle, based on the five principles, includes a vision to:

- Become a "category-of-one," company, meaning we're so good and so well known, we define the space. We want people to one day say, what's your "Pinnacle" the way they now say, let's Door-Dash that or let's Uber.

- Build a community of premium Guides, continuing to handpick and thoroughly train only the very best candidates to serve as Pinnacle Business Guides as we grow.

- Build / curate the GOAT toolbox. Our tools keep growing and that will always be the case because we evolve alongside our clients' businesses. If we don't have a necessary tool, we'll find it or build it.

I don't want to give a false impression here. Deciding on your own Pinnacle, or dream goal, then developing the strategy and systems to get you up the mountain is tough. It requires deep change and difficult decisions, no matter how good your Guide is or how clear the path, but what is the alternative? As General Eric Shinseki said, "If you don't like change, you're going to like irrelevance even less."

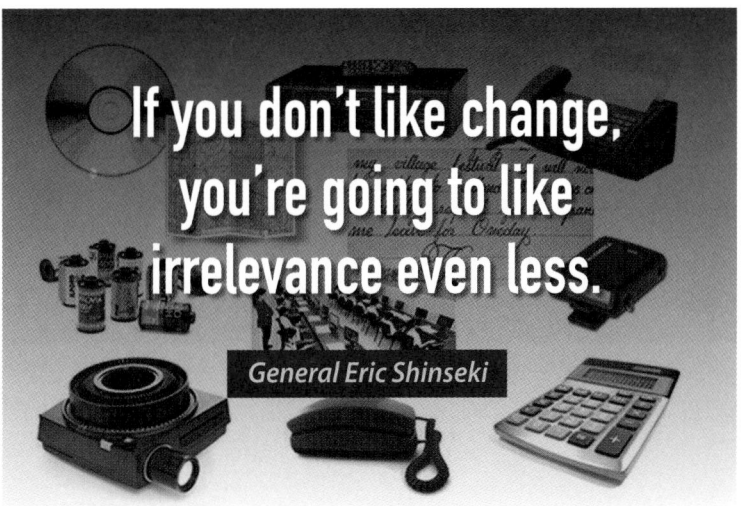

If you don't like change, you're going to like irrelevance even less.

General Eric Shinseki

As I sit at my desk writing, I'm struck by the fact that virtually nothing on it was here 15 years ago — and everything from that era has disappeared. You can descend into the same fate that befell my old fax machine, giant desktop, CDs, and calculator, or you can take a page from Steve Jobs and the latest iPhone in my pocket. Apple is on its 18th mobile operating system (that number might be higher by the time you read this) because as good as the iOS is, the company always says, you know, we can do even better.

The iPhone is great, but that ever-evolving operating system is key. The same dynamic applies in your business. You probably have terrific products or service, but that only gets you to the foothills. How good is your system? When was it last updated? As W. Edwards Deming said,

> **"** *EVERY SYSTEM IS PERFECTLY DESIGNED TO GET THE RESULTS IT GETS."*

In other words, you are earning the exact amount of profit that the system you have in place is designed to produce, whether that design is intentional or not. If you want greater Profits, stronger culture, better employee and client experiences, you must rise above your system to assess how various processes and the team members who own them are working — and then, improve it.

At Pinnacle Business Guides, we believe that the best way to build a better system and organizational health is to find an expert who can help you rise above the system and see what's really happening through the lens of five key principles: People, Purpose, Playbooks, Performance, and Profits.

The most important of these, without a doubt, is People, which is why we start our ascent to the Pinnacle with "People First" in Chapter 2.

MOUNTAIN LOOKBACK

- **OPERATING SYSTEMS.** An operating system is a prepackaged framework that helps organizations improve operations with various tools and methods.

- **GUIDES.** A good Guide provides necessary tools, highlights possible paths, and facilitates a company's climb by extracting wisdom from the leadership team.

- **PRESCRIPTIONS VS. PRINCIPLES.** A prescriptive operating system offers a set number of tools and a standardized program, while a principles-based system is customized with flexible tools and methods. It's the difference between using medications with set schedules to treat common problems vs. focusing on diet, exercise, sleep, etc. for overall health.

- **5 PRINCIPLES.** Pinnacle captures organizational health with 5 fundamental principles and 1 vital formula: **People + Purpose + Playbooks + Performance = Profits.**

- **GUIDE-CENTRIC.** Pinnacle believes in the primacy of the Guide. Having a top-notch expert guiding leaders up the mountain is the top priority for a successful climb.

- **ATROPHY.** If you're not ascending as a business, you're descending. Few can camp out at the same altitude indefinitely.

- **SYSTEM DESIGN.** Every business has an operating system, whether we know it or not, and as W. Edwards Deming said, "Every system is perfectly designed to get the results it gets."

- **THE CLIMB.** Stronger culture, process, and Profits require a stronger system. This necessitates rising above the current system to analyze how it's working and then making improvements.

CHAPTER 2

PEOPLE

IT ALL STARTS WITH WHO'S ON YOUR TEAM

The truck driver pulled to the side of the snowy road and tucked the keys into the visor. He locked the doors and, leaving the vehicle parked on a busy Minneapolis street, called the office to let them know he was done.

"Okay," the supervisor said, a little befuddled. "You mean for the whole afternoon? Where you at?"

"No, I mean for good," the driver said. "I'm on my way home." He told his supervisor where he'd left the truck and went on his way.

The supervisor was stunned. He shouldn't have been. The driver was in his sixties, with a history of back problems. The stress of weaving around snowbanks to carry gas cylinders through downtown Minneapolis, then hefting them off the truck and into businesses, had taken its toll. His performance had been slipping for some time.

The incident was indicative of a general need for fresh blood at Minneapolis Oxygen, or MO2, a need that the company's new president, Kevin Falconer, fully appreciated. Falconer had recently taken the reins from an older generation of family leadership. He grew up in the successful business and knew it intimately, a company founded in 1946 with one location and three employees as a distributor of industrial gasses and welding supplies. Nearly 80 years later, there were dozens of employees and multiple locations, ranging from western Wisconsin to Duluth, MN. MO2 supplies everything from oxygen for hospitals to CO_2 for breweries, as well as welding supplies and services.

As the company underwent a generational transition, it demonstrated a truth I constantly share with leaders: *What got us here, won't get us there*, meaning the people, processes, and strategies that worked well in driving us to our current summit are not adequate for a climb to the next. Hiking shoes, shorts, a canteen, and a pal are all you need for a good hike in the foothills. If you're scaling K2, you better have a climbing harness, crampons, an ice axe, and an expert guide, for starters.

Kevin is a natural leader, full of ambition and great instincts. He felt the truth of that aphorism long before he met me, and with an eye toward growth, was already hiring People who might help him achieve it. Once I came aboard as his Pinnacle Business Guide, though, we did a thorough "Talent Assessment" at Base

Camp, determining where the gaps in People were. We also explored what the mountaintop looked like for this company, its particular Pinnacle, or number-one goal. Over several days, we defined the company's Purpose and core values, too, before completing a Strategic Vision & Execution Plan.

Viewing the Talent Assessment (more on this and other People tools shortly) against the backdrop of MO2's newly defined Pinnacle, Purpose, and core values, Kevin realized that he essentially needed to start from scratch on a leadership team, one that could get his business to the Pinnacle we'd defined:

- **Finance.** The person in the finance "seat," or post, we determined, was out of his wheelhouse.
- **Operations.** Ops was being run by an heir-apparent who was close to retirement and didn't want to dig into a new set of Playbooks to systematize planning and processes.
- **Sales.** The Sales Manager, Kevin's brother-in-law Dana, had been a star salesperson who loved that job but seemed frustrated teaching others to do it.
- **Marketing.** This critical seat didn't exist.
- **People.** No single person was in charge of People, or HR, a critical gap, especially given the issues with drivers and turnover.

Over the next 18 months or so, we hired someone to take charge of hiring (the People person), as well as a marketing person — two new seats. We replaced the old guard in the finance and operations seats and brought in a new sales manager. Dana, a former Division I hockey player and dynamic salesman, returned to actual sales, where he would handle major accounts and be happy once again, scoring wins.

The hiring of new leaders was done gradually, roughly one major change per quarter, with core values, Purpose, and that

Pinnacle goal front and center (go faster than this and you risk causing more chaos than progress at most companies). We also began addressing the People issues around drivers and other frontline team members. A Pinnacle tool called Level Up was invaluable here. This is a way to identify and "coach up" the B-players who are in danger of becoming C-players but could also become A players, with the right mentoring, training, resources, etc. Not everyone can be saved, though, and those who continued to perform poorly were replaced.

For those who stayed or joined the team, Minneapolis Oxygen worked hard to improve its culture and work environment. This included everything from leaders having one-on-one quarterly conversations with team members to a refurbished employee lounge, with fresh paint, furniture, microwave, fridge, etc. Most leaders in search of growth look outside the business. Kevin had the wisdom to do internal work, too, "building the brand from the inside out" and understanding that a good customer experience starts with a good employee experience.

The results were remarkable once Kevin had the right team and systems in place, all serving that Pinnacle goal. Last year, Minneapolis Oxygen's profitability was six times greater than at the start of our journey. The organization is much healthier, team members are happier, the culture is stronger, and Kevin has the right people in the right seats, doing the right things as he scales that mountain.

START WITH PEOPLE

As you might have guessed from the title of this chapter, I think that Kevin Falconer's plan to start with People was a smart one, but in my experience, it puts him in a minority among leaders who want to grow their companies. Most leaders start with a vision, strategies, specific plans and goals as they head up the mountain. That's understandable, as business guru Jim Collins notes in *Good to Great: Why Some Companies Make the Leap...And Others Don't*. The fact that exceptional-growth leaders make People the first step in their ascent surprised him, too.

"We expected that good-to-great leaders would begin by setting a new vision and strategy," Collins writes in what has become a classic business text. "We found, instead, that they first got the right people on the bus, the wrong people off the bus, and the right people in the right seats..."[1]

> **WE EXPECTED THAT GOOD-TO-GREAT LEADERS WOULD BEGIN BY SETTING A NEW VISION AND STRATEGY. WE FOUND, INSTEAD, THAT THEY FIRST GOT THE RIGHT PEOPLE ON THE BUS, THE WRONG PEOPLE OFF THE BUS, AND THE RIGHT PEOPLE IN THE RIGHT SEATS..."**
> **—JIM COLLINS**

I have seen it again and again, at all sorts of businesses run by smart, experienced leaders: they are eager to plunge into tools, Playbooks, execution, Profit, etc. before dealing with People. There is logic in starting with those other elements, as Collins says, but it turns out that the best equipment in the world and the cleverest path will not get you up the mountain if you don't have a crack team to help you climb.

---

1 Jim Collins, *Good to Great: Why Some Companies Make the Leap... And Others Don't* (HarperCollins, 2001), 13.

There is a reason that People is first on our list of the five fundamental principles that grow your business. People are, far and away, your greatest resource — and your most complex. They offer your biggest competitive advantage, and you can begin changing them (in every sense of that word) tomorrow, for immediate impact. Changing People has been a necessity at 100 percent of the businesses I've worked with. That change might mean exits, entries, moves to new positions, and / or a change in attitudes and beliefs (when that last item, a conversion of sorts, proves too difficult, an exit is often preferrable: sometimes it's easier to change People than to change People).

WE ARE HIRING

"Sometimes it's easier to **change people** *than to* **change the people."**

These kinds of People decisions are the most difficult and important that any leader makes, which is one reason I encourage leaders to start with them — and why I spend more time on this principle than any of the others. After a lifetime of coaching, teaching, advising, and running businesses, I feel there is no area in which I'm more useful as a Guide.

I pointed this out, somewhat humorously, while doing a presentation at the Edina Country Club for Dermatologist Specialists, a medical practice based in Edina, Minnesota. The office had roughly 20 partners at that point, some in their 70s and ready to exit, others just a few years out of med school, with long runways ahead. I was nearing the end of my talk when a doc raised his hand: "Greg, can I ask you a question?" He sounded skeptical. "What do you know about dermatology?"

"Doctor, what I know about dermatology wouldn't fill a thimble," I said. "In fact, I've never even been to a dermatologist. Now, can I ask you a question?"

"Sure," he said.

"Are we sitting here at 7:30 on a Thursday night when you could all be home after a long day because you don't know enough about dermatology or because you have turnover on the scheduling desk, partners who aren't aligned, trouble recruiting nurses, and other People and process challenges?"

He smiled, acknowledging that I'd found the correct reason. I smiled right back and told him he was in luck because I was an expert on People problems and could help his business grow by solving them.

I went on to work with Dermatologist Specialists, impressing upon them from the start that they weren't really in the dermatology business. They were in the same business as my HVAC client, my fitness company, real estate developer, car dealership, and bank clients — the People business. All team leaders at all companies are in the People business — their organizations run on People, serve People, and die without People.

Once they realize this, they understand why we must begin to address our first and most important principle, People, on day one. You don't get halfway up the mountain and then think, hmm, maybe now I should start looking for a good guide, a climber with great technical skills, and someone with medical training. You won't solve your People issues on day one — some can take years — but all the more reason to start on them in Base Camp, not on the mountainside where the air's thin and supplies run low.

As I've mentioned and will repeat throughout this book, differentiating yourself — your product, service, brand, whatever it is that you do — is an absolute necessity in today's business environment, and the best way to achieve that is with People. They are your last great competitive advantage. Technology in many ways has leveled the playing field. Any great idea that starts on the West Coast is on the East Coast in a few weeks and vice versa — the latest sushi, dessert, steak sandwich, whatever. Create an innovative product, someone will buy it today and have it reverse-engineered by tomorrow. People aren't so easy to copy, which makes them your biggest differentiator.

For the vast majority of businesses, People are also the greatest expense. Look at your payroll if you're still not convinced that you have to think hard about People on day one of the journey. When you invest that cash in a leadership team like the one I work with at Discover Strength, a personal training company, you can run up the mountain. The leaders are young, energetic, and obsessed with their own personal training, which means they're obsessed with the company's mission, too. At the opposite pole are old-school banks whose leadership teams are what I call male, pale, and frail — a dozen men in their 60s and 70s. All have been on the team 15 or more years, and collectively, they don't have enough energy to run past the buffet line, much less up a mountain.

As I regularly say to CEOs: *Tell me who's on your team, and I'll tell you where you're going.*

Another reason to start with People is that of the five principles, addressing this one produces the fastest results. Finding new customers takes time. Changing processes and developing strategy is complex — even a price change can take three weeks to six months to fully analyze and introduce. But you can change your team, boost engagement, and improve service tomorrow, literally, with one motivational speech, highlighting your core values and Purpose. The hiring of one transformative A-player can resurrect a troubled department, even an entire company.

We start with People because they are the source of most problems — and the best solutions.

THE RIGHT PEOPLE

Jim Collins' observation of how great leaders begin taking companies from good to great is notable for its elegant simplicity: Get the right people on the bus, the wrong ones off, and the right people in the right seats. If that formula were as easy to implement as it sounds, though, every company would perform like Apple or Amazon.

Taking Collins' simple advice is complicated, as we'll explore, but it's important to realize how basic the general idea is at the start of your journey and to constantly weigh decisions against this fundamental metric. Does Ryan really belong on the bus? Is Leslie in the right seat? Who are we missing that I should get onboard?

I've explored and used countless tools that purport to answer such questions. They are either not very useful or so complicated as to be, well, not very useful. In frustration, we created our own tool, the Talent Assessment. The Talent Assessment graph shown here is fairly self-explanatory, but I'll briefly describe how it works.

Leaders enter the initials of team members in the far-left column of a chart, and in the next column, score them from 1–10 on how well they fit the company's culture (i.e. align with your core values, Purpose, Pinnacle goal, etc. — more on culture soon). In a third column, they score team members from 1–10 on productivity. Each person on the team is then plotted on the graph — their productivity on the X-axis, culture fit on the Y-axis.

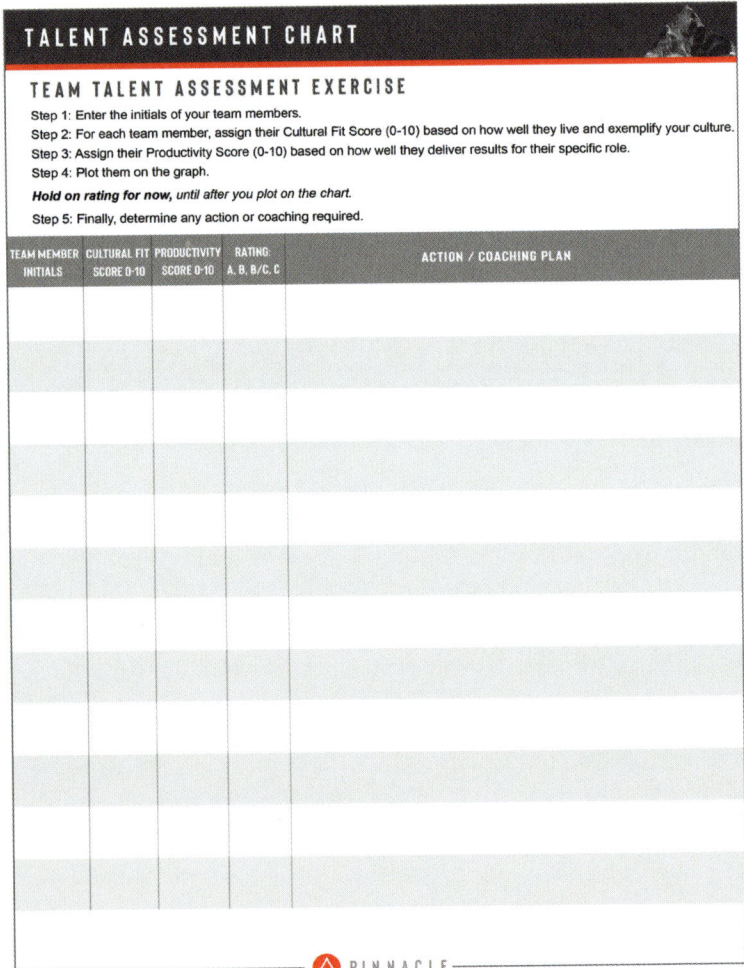

The Talent Assessment Chart is a topgrading tool that provides a clear definition of "A" players by measuring employees on a two-axis scale. The X-axis measures the productivity of the employee based on results or KPI's for their specific role. The Y-axis measures the employee based on how they live the culture of the organization.

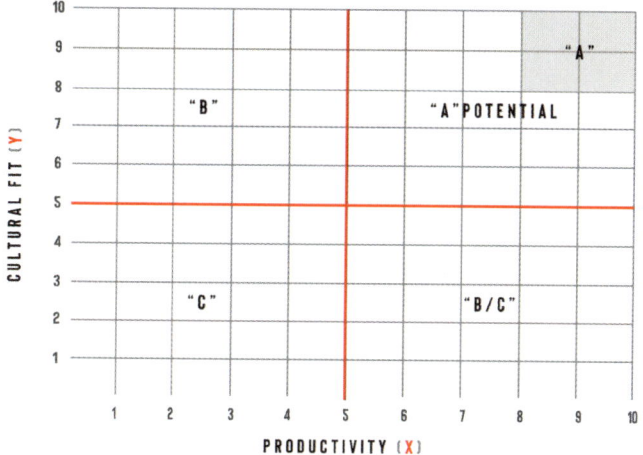

Those in the top right quadrant, scoring high on both counts, are A-players, or have A-player potential (the Climbers). Those in the top left quadrant, scoring high for culture but low for productivity, are B-players (the Campers) and need coaching up, training, mentoring, etc. Those in the bottom right square are productive and able but score low for culture (the Cranks). They should be mentored on core values and converted, if possible, though instilling belief in these misanthropes to get them up the mountain isn't easy. Those in the bottom left quadrant, scoring low for both productivity and culture are the C-players (the Cavemen). The ones who score 4 or 5 on culture and / or productivity might be coached up to become Bs or even As. The ones at the very bottom and far left are probably beyond saving and infecting the rest of your team — get them off your mountain. They'll slow your climb!

SCAN TO
DOWNLOAD

Part of the utility here is the simplicity — we can quickly rate the entire team with the two broad metrics that matter most — and see where team members are in relation to each other and our standards. The visual makes the rankings palpable, and leaders now have a language for difficult conversations: *You're a great culture fit, but your productivity needs to rise. Let's move that score from a 6 to 7 this quarter* or *You're a 9 on productivity Judy but a 3 on culture. Let's talk about core values and see if we can help you understand why this is an important...*

The Talent Assessment helps us determine who belongs on the bus. In the rest of this chapter, I'll explore the incredibly complex task tucked into Jim Collins' simple edict, but first I need to make a minor edit. On that proverbial bus, I urge leaders to get the right people in the right seats, *doing the right thing*, or, I sometimes, add *with the right boots and the right tools.*

You can have great leaders in the perfect seats, for instance, but if their objectives, goals, or mandates haven't been spelled out, you've set them up to fail. Dedicated team members at all levels quickly become deflated and unproductive if they aren't given adequate Playbooks, training, tools, or a sense of Purpose. I'll cover this piece of the equation in coming chapters, but I wanted to touch on it here because, without it, the right people in the right seats can fail as spectacularly as the wrong People in the wrong seats.

If Ben's job is to mop the factory floor, and you hand him a toothbrush, you've made it impossible for him to do the right thing. A silly example, but you get the idea. It's no less silly to tell Samantha that she owns the marketing seat but give her no staff, no budget, and no attention from the CEO. She might be the right person in the right seat, but she doesn't have the right tools, and through no fault of her own, she won't do the right thing.

Now, let's back up to consider what we mean by "the right People." Obviously, you want someone with the skills, credentials, and qualities to perform well in a particular seat. The person at the front desk should be friendly. The team member unloading hundreds of pounds of equipment probably shouldn't be five feet two inches and weigh in at 120. Maybe you want someone with a CPA in the finance seat or maybe years of experience with financials at other companies is enough. The person heading up legal should have a law degree, your sales manager extensive sales experience, and so on.

Unfortunately, leaders tend to wait until a seat is vacant to think about filling it. When that happens, they put together a brief job description and send it into the world. Three, five, or a dozen applicants reply. They interview and the best one gets the job. Congrats, you start next week!

Finding the right people is an enormous amount of work, so I understand the urge to take the best of the five, six, or a dozen candidates who showed up, even though that person isn't the best fit. *They'll figure it out, we'll manage.* Rationalizations are easy when an empty seat puts stress on systems, but that queasy feeling in your gut is usually right. In six months or a year, you'll have to pluck that square peg out of the round hole and start the painful hiring process all over again, perhaps under even more pressure (or, worse yet, the wrong person will limp along at the company, underperforming and keeping the entire team from reaching new heights).

Don't fall into traps of convenience or expediency when it comes to our first principle! People are too important. If the best of those three or 10 or 25 candidates isn't good enough, bring in the next 10, and then the next. Keep at it until you're satisfied you have the right person in the right seat.

Sifting through resumes and doing interviews is arduous, which is why I recommend a more thoughtful and strategic approach to hiring. Instead of the typical process, performed under pressure because a seat is vacant or about to be, consider the long game. We recommend our clients boil an empty seat down to the five obsessions we want that person to focus on each and every day. Having a three-page wish list, with the final catchall "and other duties as assigned" is no longer adequate. Tell prospective hires the goals and metrics they need to hit and give them the seat's four or five "obsessions." They'll have more clarity about the role and, equally important, so will you.

With such descriptions in hand and the seats in question not yet empty, leaders can hire the same way coaches recruit. No sports coach in America waits for a vacancy and then looks for someone to fill it. Coaches cultivate pipelines. They scout the competition, go to high school games, keep their eyes on the up-and-comers, make lists, and gather intelligence. They make contact as early as they can and flirt with potential team members for months, even longer. They build relationships long before they make offers, before the star players are even available, much less ready to sign. When Steve, the brilliant Vice President of Sales with your arch-rival, gets disgusted about his hours, the paltry size of his bonus, or fresh tension with his CEO, you want a seat at your company to be top of mind for him the second he considers a change — not one of 80 postings he browses after storming out of the building.

Long-term recruiting is a much healthier way to get the right people on the bus, and it makes eminent sense once you acknowledge that your business isn't really sales or manufacturing or service. Whatever you do, you are in the People business. They are your greatest differentiator and these days, your one true competitive advantage. It all starts with People. If you aren't paying close attention, it can end with them, too.

CULTURE IS KEY

The more difficult and important test for the right people is culture. A healthy business resembles a church in this regard. The "right People" are the faithful, the true believers. They believe in your Purpose, core values, and mission. They believe in your Pinnacle goal and are eager not just to do a good job, but to go the extra mile in getting the whole team up that mountain. This is, hands down, the most important criterion for "the right person."

Of course, you want someone who can hit the ground running, but skills can be taught and sharpened, training can be done on the job. Tools can be added. If someone doesn't believe, if they don't share your core values, if they're not the kind of person you want around, those deficits are unlikely to diminish.

Some leadership teams I work with, by the way, can name their core values when I ask, but many look puzzled. "We don't have core values," they say. The issue often arises as we work on the Talent Assessment at Base Camp. "Wait," someone says, "how can we do a Talent Assessment and rate for culture when we don't have core values?"

I love this question and always have my reply ready. "Of course, you have core values," I say. "You just haven't articulated them yet."

I ask leaders to name three People who have been fired because they weren't a good fit. I then ask them to name three rock stars, A-Players who would allow them to rule the world, if only they could be cloned. Well, Ryan for sure, someone says, and everyone nods. Leslie would definitely be on that list, and Julie, too. *Yes, Julie! We love her!* I probe further, asking what it is about these People that makes them such a good fit. The answers vary but might include things like *grit, tenacity, positive attitude, spirit of teamwork, character, problem-solving ability, incredible communicator, willingness to always help, goes the extra mile*...etc. We list all these qualities on the board, con-solidating and noting duplicates. What starts to emerge is the company ethos, which has been built over years.

I often compare the process of doing this exercise and using Pinnacle's Discovering Core Values tool to sculpting. David was always present in that big block of marble. It just took some chipping away on Michelangelo's part for him to emerge (the point here is not to compare myself to a great artist — though I'd love to be called the Michelangelo of business coaches — just to say that those elegant core values already exist and are ready to emerge with a little digging). We whittle down what might be 40 or 60 qualities on the board to the three to six that we all agree are vital, the values at the core of what we do, who we are, and what we stand for.

These values, when attached to behaviors and used to hire, train, and review, become powerful tools on your climb — if you truly use them. I regularly see leaders hiring "qualified" people, with the right skills, experience, and credentials who are poor fits for a company's culture. Leaders sense the gap vaguely, or spot it outright before making an offer, but then think, *well, but she has the right skills* or, *he's perfect in other ways*, as if your core values and Purpose are secondary. Believe me, they are not! All those things that make up what we refer to as "culture" create cohesion and focus. They are what get us up the mountain, as Autumn, a leader at an HVAC client of mine, recounted.

"I was giving this new service technician a tour of the facility, and we stopped at the employee lounge," she said. The company has a beautiful break area for team members, with complementary snacks and beverages. The technician cynically surmised that executives probably charged for bottled water to turn a profit — that was the sort of system he apparently was used to. "I knew at that moment he was not going to be a good culture fit," Autumn said. "I should have walked him to the nearest exit then."

> ❝ **IT'S EASY TO SPOT SKILLS. UNFORTUNATELY, CULTURE DOESN'T SHOW UP ON RESUMES."**

She didn't and, of course, nine months later — after investing in onboarding and training, as well as his share of complementary snacks — she had to fire the new guy.

Every team member must believe. Culture — your core values, Purpose, Pinnacle — is the starting point and foundation for hires, not the icing on a company cake. A lack of belief ought to be a dealbreaker every time. Unfortunately, culture doesn't show up on a resume and is difficult to detect in an interview. This is why, although we start with People, we also want our core values, Purpose, and Pinnacle goal defined when we interview and hire.

I consider Pella, the window and door company, an ideal client in this regard. When the company interviews an A-player, leaders don't simply talk about the job, they tell the story of a renowned organization. Sure, Pella is a household name and a century old, but it continues to rack up patents (150 and counting, as I write this) and prides itself on innovation. Doug Phelps, the CEO of Pella WYIDAHO, a distributorship based in Boise, Idaho, tells prospective team members that his goal is to create "a river of raving fans who flourish in life." He expounds on the idea that a healthy river is a moving river, always changing — like Pella, through its innovation — and that civilizations historically have started on rivers. He lists Pella's core values, explaining that it is "Powered by People" and "Mountain Strong," and he describes in detail the Pinnacle his team is climbing toward, driven by innovation and that river of raving fans.

Telling a powerful story like that, putting your Purpose and values on display, is an effective way to interview for culture. We can never be sure until someone is doing the work (or not), but you have a fighting chance with a candidate who gets fired up in response to such a narrative — not with lip-service, but a genuine, warm reaction. Body language alone is often a strong indicator. The interviewee who shrugs at that story or doesn't seem to get it also should be shown the nearest exit.

We'll talk more about Purpose in the next chapter, but when you make it an integral part of your hiring process, along with core values, your Pinnacle goal, and vision, the odds of hiring someone who truly believes and fits your culture go up substantially.

HIRE
A-PLAYERS

To recap, we look at three main criteria to get the right people in the right seats, doing the right thing:

Skill, Ability. Some leaders focus on this exclusively, but it's actually the easiest box to check. Put simply, can a candidate do the job? Do they have the requisite experience, skills, abilities, and credentials? A resume gives a pretty good read here.

Belief, Culture. This is not on the resume and can be tough to ascertain even in a thorough interview. Lots of People interview well, but do they really share your core values? Are they inspired to help you climb to the Pinnacle? Telling your story and sharing your Purpose, Pinnacle, and core values is a good way to determine if People are a good fit.

Tools, Training. The right people have to be in the right seats for growth, but they must also be doing the right thing. Clear communication and goals, the necessary tools, training, resources, etc. turn potential into the actual. If you don't provide what they need to succeed, the failure is yours.

No matter how diligent you are about using solid criteria to put the right People in the right seats, I estimate the chance of success at fifty-fifty for most hires. This is where the phenomenon that my client Luke Carlson, the CEO of Discover Strength, calls "the pain of people." Humans are unpredictable at the best of times. No matter how much you have done for someone, hiring, training, and investing in them, the mountain passes are littered with disappointments, betrayals, dropped equipment, and abandoned maps. Everyone in business has suffered setbacks and even tragedies at the hands of fellow humans. Every leader suffers sleepless nights because someone doesn't deliver, absconds, steals, misrepresents things, or outright lies.

Starting in the modest place I did in life, I have realized more success that anyone could have predicted, helped at every stage of my career by talented, hardworking people. I have also been stabbed in the back more than once. I've gone to bat for people, loaned them money, paid their bills, built businesses with them, taught them all I could — and then had them leave without warning, refuse to honor deals, or loot whatever wasn't bolted down.

Every entrepreneur learns this lesson, and it's an important one to keep in mind — People will disappoint you, love them anyway. They will let you down and hurt you, love them anyway. What choice do you have? None of us exists in solitude, and you can't get up that mountain on your own. You have to rely on others, and that means making yourself vulnerable. An old Japanese proverb instructs, "Fall down seven times, stand up eight." This is what matters as you address the most important of our five fundamental principles. No matter how bad the pain of People gets, how many disappointments you suffer, stand back up, invest again, trust again. Stay true to your Purpose and core values, treat People well, and enough of them will come through to get you up the mountain.

As I write this, Pinnacle Business Guides has hired five people in the last six weeks. I hope they're all A-players — I'm paying them as if they are — but my odds on each of these carefully placed bets are just 50/50. That's right, the guy who's adamant about hiring for culture as well as skill, who researches and lectures on the subject, whose whole business revolves around the effective recruitment, hiring, training, and management of People bats 500.

But as most entrepreneurs know, 500 would be a superhuman batting average in baseball, and it's a great record in business, too. The first marketing person we hired at Minneapolis Oxygen, the example I related at the start of this chapter, didn't work out and neither did the first person in the company's People seat, but in each of those cases, we got the second hire right — a good result.

Understanding the enormous challenge of People decisions and the fact that we all sometimes get them wrong helps with two vital elements of your climb. First, it allows you to recognize a poor choice, forgive yourself, make a quick correction, and stand back up — rather than working with that poor choice for years. Second, it highlights the benefit of going after A-Players. Trying for the very best increases your odds. You'll still fail, but you will also succeed, sometimes spectacularly.

A-players pay for themselves. Most readers know what I mean by A-players, but to be clear, these are highly skilled and experienced People who do their jobs and embrace your culture, but more than that, they also love the challenge of your Pinnacle goal and will do whatever they humanly can to get the team up that mountain. They work tirelessly and creatively in that effort, and this is why, although they often cost more, they pay for themselves. They contribute more than they take.

Spending another $10,000, $20,000, or $200,000, depending on company size, for an A-player is a smart investment — you will make that money back (how much would it be worth to have Sheryl Sandberg, Bill Gates, or Meg Whitman in a corner office?). More important than the bottom line, though, is the outsized effect of adding an A-player to the team. The A-player is like a snowball rolling up the mountain while others trudge, growing in size and momentum with every foot of elevation. This hiring strategy, according to Steve Jobs, was the secret behind much of his achievement.

"I've built a lot of my success off finding these truly gifted people and not settling for B and C-players..." Jobs said. "I found that when you get enough A-players together, when you go through the incredible work to find five of these A-players, they really like working with each other... and they don't want to work with B- and C-players, and so it becomes self-policing, and they only want to hire more A players, so you build up these pockets of A players, and it propagates."[2]

A-players lift up and inspire other team members. Michael Jordan didn't win all those championships and take the Bulls to their Pinnacle simply by making incredible shots and scoring 30 points a game. He worked hard to learn Phil Jackson's system, the famous triangle offense that gave every player the chance to touch the ball and score. Jordan's belief in that system put winning above his sizeable, fully warranted ego. He gave the game his all and inspired his fellow players, who knew he relied on them, to deliver their best.

> *" I'VE BUILT A LOT OF MY SUCCESS OFF FINDING THESE TRULY GIFTED PEOPLE AND NOT SETTLING FOR B AND C-PLAYERS...I FOUND THAT WHEN YOU GET ENOUGH A-PLAYERS TOGETHER, WHEN YOU GO THROUGH THE INCREDIBLE WORK TO FIND FIVE OF THESE A-PLAYERS, THEY REALLY LIKE WORKING WITH EACH OTHER...AND THEY DON'T WANT TO WORK WITH B AND C-PLAYERS, AND SO IT BECOMES SELF-POLICING, AND THEY ONLY WANT TO HIRE MORE A-PLAYERS, SO YOU BUILD UP THESE POCKETS OF A-PLAYERS, AND IT PROPAGATES."*
> —STEVE JOBS

I watched this A-player team dynamic firsthand with my son, Ben, over the years as he went from high school hockey to the University of Tampa Spartans (a team that as I type this just won its first national championship). He was talented from a young age and always had the option to play up or down a level.

---

2   Steve Jobs, *Steve Jobs: The Lost Interview,* May 11, 2012 (interview conducted in 1995 with Robert X. Cringley).

I would say, "Ben, if you play at your level you can be a star, get on the ice all the time, score a kajillion goals." Without fail, he replied, "Dad, I'd rather be the worst guy on the best team because they're going to make me better." As a high schooler, he practiced with the college kids all summer because, like other A-players, he wanted to be challenged and up his game.

The inverse dynamic also holds. Steve Jobs famously said that A-players hire A-players, B-players hire C-players and with enough C-players at a company, pretty soon, you have "a bozo explosion." Avoid the bozo explosion! People are your last competitive advantage and chief differentiator. Now more than ever, it makes sense to invest in the best of them.

TIME TO LEVEL UP

Lethargy, indifference, and incompetence spread more quickly than excellence, unfortunately, and your C-players will give their bug to B-players while deeply annoying the A-players. It's important to identify the C-players hurting your team and, as Jim Collins advised, get them off the bus.

The B-players present a more difficult case, and how you deal with them is a major factor in achieving organizational health. Every B-player is in danger of becoming a C-player, and it's imperative that you reach them before that slide. Pinnacle Business Guides use a tool called "Level Up" to identify the B-players who can be turned into A-players by coaching them up to the next level. I'll explain this tool and another useful People tool, "The Draft," in a moment. First, though, I want to point out that many B-players are actually A-players stuck in the wrong seats.

We saw this sort of misplacement in the story I told at the start of this chapter. The star salesman at Minneapolis Oxygen, was put in the sales manager seat. Over time, he went from happy and excelling to frustrated and miserable. I see similar examples of the right people in the wrong seats at every level of the organizations I work with. One version of this phenomenon is the famous Peter principle, which holds that People tend to rise to the level of their own incompetence. An incredibly skilled technician, installer, salesperson, etc. is yanked out of the field and made a supervisor or manager. They do well at this job, so they're promoted to regional manager, a job at which they truly suck. The promotions stop there because their performance doesn't warrant another. They have reached the level of their incompetence and, with the Peter principle in full effect, will limp along an uncomfortable plateau.

Tenure alone is not a good reason to promote someone, much less put them on a leadership team. Beware the heir apparent! The fact that Russ is your second cousin is an even worse reason for promotion, and no one should get a spot on the leadership team simply because you bought their company. Such promotions are the fault of leaders, not those promoted, but they often result in the kind of firing Patrick Lencioni calls "the last act of cowardice" for its lack of warning.

It's much harder to communicate clearly, to offer the mentoring, training, tools, and resources that might give Russ a fighting chance in his seat. If such measures don't work, it's worth exploring why and, if warranted, reversing the Peter Principle. It is difficult to go from Vice President of Marketing back to Marketing Manager, or from Marketing Manager to Copywriter, but sometimes it's the right move. Such a shift can work if the relationships are strong and affected team members are on board.

Of course, it's better not to get to the point where the alternatives are firing or demotion. As leaders, we want to be smoke detectors, not firemen. We need to be clear-eyed about Performance and have the hard conversations early, especially when we have the potential to turn B-players into top performers.

I created this Level Up tool to help leaders spot those B-players and coach them up a level. The exercise contains just five questions followed by a discussion. The first two questions ask leaders to assess themselves, to demonstrate that we all have room for improvement and to encourage an honest assessment of team members in the next three queries. Each question builds on the previous one, and they get harder as we progress.

LEVEL UP

2 Strengths. Ask leaders to name two places where they're performing well in their leadership role.

2 Improvements. Emphasizing that we all have room for improvement, ask leaders to name two areas where they need to do better as leaders.

Underperformers. Assuring everyone that this is not a witch hunt and no one's getting fired, ask leaders to list the underperformers on their teams. No reasons, excuses, or context allowed — just the names. If the Pareto Principle, or 80-20 rule, holds (it's nearly infallible), out of 100 team members, 20 will be underperforming. Put those names on the board. As an aside, note how big the payroll is for this list.

Save or Don't. This question is hard, and the answer must be a quick gut-check — no agonizing or debates. Go through the names on each leader's team, asking how they would feel tomorrow if Russ quit. How about Ryan? Leslie? Steve? Of 20 underperformers, there are usually five or six who leaders would be upset to see quitting, who they want to save. *No,* they say, *she just hasn't had enough training* or *I need to spend a little more time with him* or *he has great potential even though...*But for 13 or 14 names, leaders say, *Not only would I be okay if they quit, I feel relieved just thinking about it. They've been here a long time, and I don't know what to do with them...*

Rockstars. Finally, ask who the rock stars are. Give leaders some time, then list the names they call out on the board (again, the 80-20 rule predicts 20 stars for every 100 team members). Ask how leaders would react if these People came in tomorrow and said they needed more money or they'd have to walk. Every leader will say some version of, *I give the raise...I write a check...I get finance on the phone...*They know in their gut that these A-players are free. They are the seed corn that must be preserved, or the company won't have a crop next year.

Any time there is a need to have a conversation regarding the "Right People in the Right Seats." This is a great way to get those conversations on the table.

QUESTION 1 What are two areas where you feel you are performing well in your role as a leader in this company?

QUESTION 2 What are two areas where you feel you are UNDERperforming in your role as a leader in this company? You know in your heart and soul you can and should be doing a better job.

PINNACLE

Follow up the questions with a discussion, asking leaders to review the names on the board and pick out who they spend the most time on. Is it the rockstars or the People whose exit would spell relief? How and where should they be spending their time? What sort of mentoring, training, or resources can turn those B-players worth saving into A-players?

The Level Up exercise highlights the value of A-players, who are free and too often underappreciated, and the burden of C-players, whose exit at the next bus stop would make their bosses sleep easier. Most important, it shines a light on the B-players who have potential, whose exit might be a loss, but who need additional time, training, conversations, etc. if they are to up their game and not slide into C-player terrain.

Leaders love this tool for the clarity it brings to Performance — and the aha it leads to regarding their biggest expense, payroll. When I introduced this exercise to GCI, the San Francisco-based commercial general contractor, I'd written the names of 14 underperformers on the whiteboard when CEO Jon Hellman

stopped me. "Greg," he said, "If we go through these 14 people and clearly articulate why they're on the list, what specifically can get them off it, and who's going to take action on those things, that would be the most incredible use of our time I can think of."

Level Up is normally a one-hour exercise, but we spent the rest of the day analyzing and crafting a Level Up plan for each person on the list. It worked so well, GCI has built this customized tool into its annual schedule.

Another Pinnacle tool, The Draft, approaches personnel questions from another angle, highlighting costs, benefits, teamwork, balance, and a host of other patterns. This might sound like dull, difficult analysis, but the exercise, which we do at our Annual Summits, is possibly the most fun in the toolbox. Here's how it works:

THE DRAFT

As you might have guessed from the name, The Draft treats your company like a fantasy sports team and works the same way. We start by saying, okay, we're going to build a new _____ company, starting from scratch (fill in the blank with construction, financial services, restaurant, bank, or whatever your business does). If there are seven people on the leadership team, we announce that we're going to draft about half the company, going seven rounds deep. We let leaders choose their draft pick order and do a "snake" draft, meaning if someone picks a "player" last in the first round, they will then pick first in the second round, and so on, snaking through the draft until all roster spots are filled.

The exercise is fun, with no pressure and lots of laughs — I play the Jeopardy theme music, to give you a feel for the tone — but leaders also get competitive and strategic about assembling the best possible team from scratch. In a discussion afterwards, we go over what people were thinking and why they made various choices. What was your mindset as you made these picks? Why did the "utility" People, with very specific skills, go so quickly? Whose team has the best culture fit? Who broke the salary cap? Who put together a team of misfits or the one most challenging for company culture? Okay, you nabbed three alphas, but those People are never going to get along on the same team...

The observations and patterns can be quite revealing. Who, for instance, remains a free agent and why? Did some supervisors or managers not get picked? This is a question worthy of discussion. If no one from a particular office or location got drafted, what does that say? We do this exercise each year, and the annual trends can be illuminating. Samantha was round five last year, and she went round one this year — big progress — whereas Sergui moved in the opposite direction. Of course, such shifts are marked with arrows pointing up or down...

After all of the laughs and quips — we're on our way to dinner when we put this tool back in the box — leaders leave with real intelligence about their teams and plenty of food for thought.

Purpose is an important part of our Draft discussions, and it's also at the heart of the Talent Assessment and Level Up tools introduced here. As I hope I made clear in our discussion of culture, aligning People with Purpose is a necessity for anyone hoping to grow. But how do leaders establish and communicate a clear Purpose, demonstrating how they're different? How do we make the concept concrete and use it not just in hiring, but also in strategy, planning, and our daily work? In Chapter 3, we'll explore how Purpose is a part of every breath champion climbers draw, spurring them to ever greater heights.

MOUNTAIN LOOKBACK

- **Start with People.** People are your greatest resource and biggest competitive advantage. Vision and strategy are meaningless without them, so start with People.

- **The People Business.** We are all in the same business, whatever your industry — the People business.

- **Right People, Right Seats.** Get the right People on the bus, as Jim Collins says, the wrong ones off, and the right People in the right seats with the right tools.

- **Fastest Results.** Of our 5 principles, working on People produces the fastest results. You can boost engagement and improve service tomorrow with one motivational speech. Hiring one A-player can quickly change a department or even company.

- **Talent Assessment.** Use a simple metric with a visual component like our Talent Assessment to rate team members for productivity and culture. The "right People" score high in both.

- **Recruit Long-term.** Cultivate a talent pipeline, like a sports coach. Scout competition, build relationships, and watch up-and-comers. Think of hiring as a long-term process, not short-term filling of vacancies.

- **Culture is Key.** Make your Purpose and core values key criteria in hiring, training, and coaching. The "right People" have necessary skills and credentials — and align with your culture.

- **Hire A-Players.** Team members who are highly skilled and productive, who embrace your culture and go the extra mile, are free because they give more than they take. A-players propagate A-players; C-players lead to a "bozo explosion."

- **Level Up.** Coach your B-players into A-players and C-players into B-players, if possible. If not, get them off the bus.

- **Communicate Clearly.** Spot and address issues early: be a smoke detector, not a firefighter.

CHAPTER 3

PURPOSE

Doug Phelps worked for Pella, the top brand for windows and doors, in the company's home state of Iowa for 22 years before buying an Idaho distributorship in 2023.

Actually, "carving out" might be a better descriptor than "buying." He purchased the southern Idaho portion of a territory that also included all of Utah and Arizona. Pella, which celebrated a century in business in 2025, has a rich tradition, but Doug was now leading a newly independent entity he hoped to grow in a state that was also new, at least to him. If he was going to be successful, he thought, he had to start by establishing a clear Purpose and direction for Pella WYIDAHO.

"We really needed to spend time establishing who we were and why we existed and what our goals were," he said. "That was our biggest priority, even more than sales, to really immerse ourselves in the culture and our strategic direction for the company, so we all understood where we're trying to go."

When I came aboard as Pella WYIDAHO's Guide, Doug's attitude was as inspiring to me as I knew his Purpose and Pinnacle, or number-one goal, would be to his team. After People, Purpose is the most important of our five fundamental principles and yet, it's frequently neglected, even ignored by leaders. For some companies, this is because they truly don't have a Purpose — they stand for nothing. If that's the case, they'll never get up the mountain. Others have a Purpose but don't take it seriously or enlist it in their climb — its usefulness never reaches past a plaque at the reception desk or a website landing page.

But leaders like Doug Phelps understand that Purpose directs everything. They would no sooner attempt build a business without a clearly articulated Purpose than experienced moun-taineers would climb K2 without a working compass. Doug was already building his compass and searching for the ascending path when I arrived. As I've said, my job as a Guide is simply to help leaders find the trail that's been there all along, though it may be buried under snow and fallen leaves, to facilitate the climb.

Using several Pinnacle tools, we worked hard to get Pella WYIDAHO's Purpose right. Doug and other leaders shaped and reshaped it. I challenged each Purpose statement, prodding at its truth, meaning, and language.

Finally, the company decided its Purpose is *To create a river of raving fans who flourish in life*. Pella WYIDAHO's Pinnacle, or number-one goal, became *To deliver extraordinary experiences for everyone* — E3, for short. We'll explore the differences between Purpose and a Pinnacle goal shortly. For now, think of Purpose as the overarching lifetime thing the business will always strive to accomplish, while the Pinnacle is subsidiary, a bold, ambitious but shorter-term target that helps fulfill the larger one.

In case Pella WYIDAHO's Purpose strikes readers as merely pretty words, I'll briefly explain it. "Raving fans" refers to employees, customers, and the community overall. Doug explains that simply doing a good job doesn't create a "raving fan" — for that, you must provide an *extraordinary experience*, his goal for every interaction (already, as you can see, we're connecting Purpose and the Pinnacle goal of E3). Those fans are visualized as a river partly because, although it's high desert, Idaho and Wyoming are laced with vital rivers, and partly because rivers are a source of nourishment and abundance. What does "flourish" mean in the business context? It implies growth and prosperity, sure, but it's different for everyone. For a particular customer, getting a service they can't find elsewhere or extra flexibility might help them to flourish. For one employee, flourishing might mean income or career advancement, and for another, a meaningful way to give back to the community.

"You have to build really good relationships and ask great questions about what *flourish in life* means to them," Doug says, "because everyone defines that differently."

As you can see from Pella WYIDAHO's Purpose, this principle is closely related to our first principle, People. For Doug — a man of deep faith — it has become a touchstone for every interaction, guiding how he and everyone in the business should treat customers and each other. It's also the base on which his vision, goals, and strategy are built — a connection most business operating systems miss. They're good at helping to decide on a destination, but how to get there? Not so much.

That disconnect between Purpose and strategy is one reason so many leaders don't truly embrace the second of the five fundamental principles. To them, it looks like an accessory or empty exercise, not a climbing tool. Our clients understand that Purpose is an engine, not just an idea, because we tie it to strategy, goals, and daily operations.

At Pella WYIDAHO, the company's Purpose and Pinnacle goal steer strategic decisions like a compass as team members trek up the mountain. To give one example, the business moved functions that had been outsourced, such as scheduling service and deliveries, back in-house because it's hard to create raving fans and deliver an extraordinary experience for everyone if you don't control every piece of that experience.

Pella WYIDAHO's Purpose and Pinnacle goal also motivate and inspire team members, providing a powerful base for the company's culture, and differentiating Pella WYIDAHO from the competition. They are at the heart of every meeting, a key part of hiring and reviewing employees, and maybe most important for a rapidly growing company, they provide alignment and autonomy for all team members.

"Purpose is really important as you're growing. We're moving fast, and we want our employees to be able to make decisions within the scope of their roles and not have to check with someone all the time," Doug says, noting that he went from 33 team members to more than 60 in less than two years. "Knowing why we exist as a company, what our values are, really guides the interactions that we have with customers, but also with each other. That's been the most fun part of this, I would say — getting everybody aligned and then just watching people out there making decisions and improving the business without a whole lot of extra guidance from me."

This is music to a Pinnacle Business Guide's ears because it's a major part of *our* Purpose — developing People, Purpose, Playbooks, and Performance, so that the business runs like a well-oiled machine, giving leaders the time and space to lead and boost Profits.

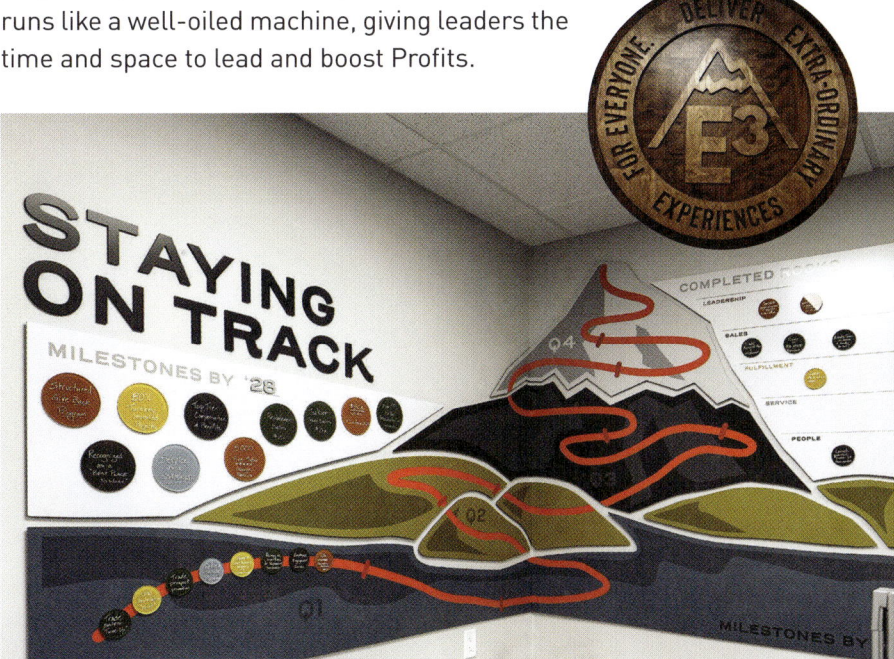

DEFINING YOUR *WHY*

The word "Purpose" gets thrown around a lot in business circles these days, often without much conviction, so before we proceed, I want to explain exactly what I mean by it.

The *Purpose* of your business is the reason it exists. Your Purpose captures what you stand for and who you are. For your entire team, it answers the question, *Where are we headed?* Like most process fanatics, I'm a fan of simplicity, so I often use a lunch date as an example on that last question. If I ask you to lunch, you only need two pieces of information — where are we going and when? So much of success in business comes down to understanding these two fundamentals: Where are you going? When will you get there?

Whatever your destination, Purpose is your compass or North Star on that journey. The North Star, of course, is the brightest star in its constellation and has been used by sailors, explorers, and mountaineers for millennia to find due north, to understand where they are and the direction they need to travel. Its brightness and stable position in the northern sky make it ideal for navigation.

The same is true of Purpose. Like the North Star or a good compass, it gives you a sense of where you are and where you're going as you head up the mountain. It helps you navigate and as you share it with your team, it orients each of them. If team members aren't all facing in the same direction, you have chaos, not a successful climb, which is why smart leaders make Purpose a priority at Base Camp, before the ascent — not after they've wandered onto a mountainside cliff, directionless.

I'll delve into the finer aspects of Purpose in a bit, but it should be permanent, aspirational, inspiring, and authentic to who you are as an organization. As I noted above, most companies have one Purpose for their entire existence. If your Purpose changes every year, or even each decade, you don't have one. A true Purpose is timeless. It should also be authentic, meaning particular to you. You'd like to double your income? So would most companies — nothing authentic or unique about it. If you're including a dollar sign in your Purpose, start over.

The best Purpose statements, in my experience, involve making the world a better place. Most, like Pella WYIDAHO's, don't even mention the product or service that the business sells. When Pete and Lucille Kuyper began growing Pella in the town of Pella, Iowa in the mid-1920s, Pete said, "Our broadest conception of success is measured by the influence for good with our neighbors." Long before companies formally thought about "Purpose statements," Kuyper had a good one — big, authentic, and inspiring.

While we're on Pella, another client of mine, Pella Northland, which covers Minnesota and Fargo, North Dakota, has a brilliantly articulated Purpose that doesn't explicitly mention windows as a product but references them much more expansively. The company's Purpose is *To improve people's view of the world and their place in it.*

I've been at this a long time, and it doesn't get much better than this! Sure, windows provide views, so the Purpose makes literal sense for this company, but in framing the idea (pun intended) as "people's view of the world" Pella Northland implies customers' whole outlook and even happiness, not just what they can see of their block through a pane of glass. Turning that view around — "and their place in it" — continues this theme. Your first apartment or townhouse probably has small windows and a poor view. As you get on in life, your house and windows likely expand, and even if you remain in a condo, you hope to be on a higher floor with a better view over time. Pella Northland pledges to help you improve and enjoy those views every step of the way.

I remember working hard on this with Pella Northland leaders, struggling to clearly state a Purpose we all felt but couldn't adequately express. Melissa, the leader in charge of operations, suddenly said, I think I've got it. She uttered what's now the company's Purpose, and everyone said, yep, that's it. Such a reaction is common. When you finally uncover that authentic, inspiring Purpose, it's an *aha* moment. Yes, we think, perfect! If your Purpose doesn't feel like an epiphany, you're not there yet.

This is another reason why money isn't relevant here. Your Purpose should inspire the entire team, guide and motivate everyone from the delivery drivers and receptionist to the CEO. A Purpose of growing revenue to $300 million might inspire ownership, but it's not going to drive the entire team to greater heights. No admin arrives at work early because he's dying to make more money for the boss, but if he works at Toms Shoes, that company's Purpose — *Use business to improve lives* — might very well inspire him, especially once he knows that Toms has given away 100 million pairs of shoes and counting to those in need…

Here are some other examples of exemplary Purpose statements from great companies we all know.

Note that of the seven examples on the right, only two directly mention a product — Southwest and Starbucks (and the coffee part of Starbucks' Purpose is a recent change). Nike mentions athletes, cleverly telling customers that they are all athletes, but doesn't flog shoes. Instead, the company's mission is centered on inspiration and innovation. Southwest promotes low-cost air travel — its forte — but highlights the idea of connecting people to the things they care about. What's more likely to get employees out of bed in the morning: "Connecting people to what's important in their lives" or "Cheap flights for all?"

 **Nike.** To bring inspiration and innovation to every athlete* in the world. (*If you have a body, you are an athlete.)

 **Airbnb.** To create a world where anyone can belong anywhere.

 **Southwest Airlines.** To connect people to what's important in their lives through friendly, reliable, and low-cost air travel.

 **Netflix.** To entertain the world.

 Uber. To ignite opportunity by setting the world in motion.

 **Zappos.** To live and deliver WOW!

 **Starbucks.** To be the premiere purveyor of the finest coffee in the world, inspiring and nurturing the human spirit one person, one cup, and one neighborhood at a time.

 **LinkedIn.** To connect the world's professionals to make them more productive and successful.

WHY FOCUS ON *WHY*?

I'll provide tips later on how to craft your own powerful Purpose statement, but first, I want to explore the purpose of Purpose, the reason for stating the reason you exist. If as a Guide, I tell leaders they must know and communicate their *why*, I should say, well, *why* that's the case. This is crucial, I think, because everyone running a business appreciates sales, revenue, goals, process, systems...But Purpose? It can seem comparatively esoteric and ethereal, disconnected from day-to-day operations.

It isn't.

Purpose is a key part of getting your business to run smoothly, so that you can focus on the climb. It's also how you decide which peak you're climbing toward and how you'll get there. Yes, Purpose is idealistic but it's also strategic and utterly practical, as important to your company as a steering wheel is to your car. Here are some of the broad areas where it's most useful:

- **Direction.** I've compared Purpose to a compass because it helps you decide where you're going. Done right, it's also strategic, helping you decide how to get there.

- **Alignment.** Just as Purpose helps leaders define the company's direction, it also helps workers at all levels make daily decisions, staying focused and united in a common effort.

- **Inspiration.** Purpose helps everyone on the team find meaning in their work, improving engagement and Performance by meeting this basic human need.

- **Culture.** Purpose sets you apart from the competition, building trust and loyalty among customers and team members. It's where everything termed "culture" — organizational values, beliefs, behaviors, etc. — begins.

Your Pinnacle — that bold, number-one goal — is useful in similar ways, though with a shorter time horizon. Before I address the categories above in detail, let's take a moment to think about Pinnacle goals, how they differ from and work in concert with Purpose.

Your Purpose is permanent, but as I've said, a company might have several Pinnacles over its lifespan. For my clients, the typical Pinnacle goal has a timeframe of five to seven years. In *Built to Last: Successful Habits of Visionary Companies*, Jim Collins and Jerry Porras called this sort of target a "big hairy audacious goal," or BHAG, a trademarked term that's become a staple of business parlance.

Purpose is who you are and why you exist. A Pinnacle goal describes a peak worthy of the climb, a target everyone in the organization can rally behind and work toward in the short-er-term while delivering on Purpose long-term. I am a big fan of Joseph Campbell, author of *The Hero with a Thousand Faces* and chronicler of what he called "the hero's journey." Announc-ing the Pinnacle that you're climbing toward at an organization is like the call to adventure Campbell described as the start of the hero's journey, kicking off the epic quest for your version of a holy grail or golden fleece.

There is something primal and tribal about this sort of quest (or climb, as we say), which is at the root of so much human struggle. It explains the appeal of everything from *Star Wars* to modern sports rivalries, and it's an incredible way to energize your team.

I'll give a couple quick examples, so you are clear on the differ-ence between Pinnacle and Purpose. The Purpose of SpaceX is *To make life multi-planetary*. Its Pinnacle goal is to colonize Mars. The company plans to send a number of uncrewed Starships to Mars in 2026, with a crewed mission to follow in four years. The Pinnacle helps deliver on the larger Purpose. It's also bold, ambitious, and clearly, a great way to capture imagination and fire up the troops.

At Pinnacle Business Guides, our Purpose is *To positively impact lives — one Guide, one client, one mountain at a time.* This will always be our Purpose. It is an overarching ideal standard we'll always strive to meet. Our Pinnacle goal — *the Pinnacle Pinnacle,* you might say — is *To become the brand against which all others will be judged.* Our Purpose is why we exist and get out of bed each morning. Our Pinnacle is what the mountaintop looks like for us, the thing we rally behind, cheer for, and hope to achieve in five to seven years.

Because we live in an experience economy — it's all UX, Google Reviews, and value-adds — most of my clients aim for experiential Pinnacles. They want to create exceptional, extraordinary, or elevated *experiences* for their customers. They can't compete with massive corporations on volume or with tech companies on innovations that demand serious R&D, but they can compete quite effectively on experience.

Your Pinnacle and Purpose work hand-in-hand, but Purpose is steering the ship.

Now that we've made that distinction, let's return to those broad categories where Purpose can have a powerful impact.

▎DIRECTION

Purpose, as I've said, serves as a compass for leaders as they set out to climb, helping them decide on a direction and the best paths — think strategies — up the mountain. How does Purpose connect to strategy? I mentioned one example early in this chapter, and it's worth repeating.

Pella WYIDAHO's Purpose — *To create a river of raving fans who flourish in life* — left no doubt in leaders' minds that the company had to return outsourced functions, such as scheduling service and deliveries, in-house. The business could not consistently create raving fans and deliver an extraordinary experience for everyone when important points of customer contact were out of its control. Purpose made this an easy decision and led to tangible strategy. The company would have to hire a significant number of new team members to provide those services in-house. That hiring became a vital part of its Strategic Vision & Execution Plan and resulted in concrete goals, milestones, and quarterly "Rocks" (the 90-day priorities leading to those larger goals). It all starts with People, as I said in the last chapter, but followed closely by Purpose.

Our Purpose, as I've said, is *To positively impact lives — one Guide, one client, one mountain at a time.* To provide that level of service, we have to recruit top-notch Guides — people with long experience, deep expertise, flexibility, and empathy. We want to be a category-of-one company, the brand against which all others will be judged. That second goal — our Pinnacle — demands growth, but the high standard dictated by our Purpose (top-notch Guides only) regulates and shapes that growth. Our Purpose in this case helps us turn down anyone who is not an absolute A-player despite our desire to grow. This is an important hallmark of Purpose — it helps you to say no.

Our Purpose is noble, I hope, but as you can see, it's also concrete and strategic. As I write this, our annual growth plan calls for 200 Guides by the end of 2025. That vision and its attendant strategy — milestones, goals, quarterly Rocks, etc. — grew directly out of and was shaped by our Purpose. Purpose gives us direction not just in some vague, idealized sense but by influencing strategic planning and decision-making every day, quarter, year. After decades of running and coaching businesses, I'm utterly comfortable drafting growth plans, but working on a plan without a Purpose would feel like sketching on a whiteboard blindfolded. Whatever I thought I was putting up there for leaders would look sloppy and soon, nonsensical — a map for chaos, not a climb.

Purpose also serves as a powerful compass for frontline workers, middle managers — the entire team — when it's baked into the company. Yes, we want it on those signs at the reception desk and the lunchroom, on letterhead, coffee cups, and the website, but we also want to make our Purpose the heart of every meeting and a vital part of hiring, training, and reviewing employees in order to help everyone face the same way and make good decisions.

The Purpose of Minneapolis Oxygen, the company that sells industrial gasses, mentioned in Chapter 2, is: *Together we make a difference.* That purpose is embedded in the brain of every team member, and faced with a decision, each now has a compass offering direction at forks in the trail. Is the choice I'm making the right one for the team? Will it make a positive difference, however small, in the climb we've undertaken together? Does this move go against our Purpose or core values? MO2's *why* offers a constant gut check, a way to say yes or no, without running everything by leaders.

▍ ALIGNMENT

Minneapolis Oxygen, like most companies, has suffered its share of personnel issues, also has built alignment by showing team members that leadership takes the company's Purpose, *Together we make a difference,* seriously. MO2 has worked hard to improve the employee experience and boost support, assigning 90-day mentors, holding quarterly coaching conversations, and having weekly "Level Up" tactical meetings to help B-players improve. The boost to morale and embrace of core values created by Minneapolis Oxygen's integration of a powerful Purpose is impressive.

Like the movement of a flywheel (a favorite metaphor at Pinnacle), the dynamic at MO2 is wonderfully circular and full of momentum. Purpose led to the company's new employee supports and is now embedded within them. Mentors and leaders discuss how team members have delivered on the idea that *Together we make a difference* in those quarterly coaching conversations and weekly Level Up tacticals. Taken seriously, Purpose creates mechanisms that reinforce Purpose as we climb.

Minneapolis Oxygen also strives to hire people who will align with its Purpose, as does Pella WYIDAHO, though it took a little time to integrate this standard into the company's talent acquisition. The gap became apparent as we went over Pella WYIDAHO's Talent Assessment at a Quarterly Summit. When I asked about culture, Doug Phelps noted that several employees weren't scoring well.

"How is that possible?" I asked him and the other leaders gathered. "These are new hires, right, brought on after all your work on culture? What questions are you asking when you interview to make sure they align with your Purpose and core values?"

I could almost see the lightbulb switching on above Doug's head.

"We looked at each other, and we had a learning moment," he said later. "Of course, we weren't asking the right questions. Now, we talk to applicants about who we are in the interviews. We explain our mission and vision and ask questions about how they'd respond to certain situations and challenges to understand whether they align with our Purpose and values."

Team members who align with your Purpose and embrace the company's core values have what, in a religious context, we call faith, and the value of that commodity to the organization and its mission is hard to overstate. I don't know if faith can move mountains, but it's an absolute necessity if you want to climb one.

Our Mission   **Our Values**   **Our Vision (#1 Goal)**

▌INSPIRATION

As leaders, we want true believers helping us up the mountain, for their benefit as well as ours, but if you don't have a solid Purpose, you'll never find them. Talented, ambitious, bright People — young People especially, but all People — want meaning in their lives. They want to be inspired. This, as Viktor Frankl so eloquently pointed out in *Man's Search for Meaning*, is a basic human need, the desire to do something important in the world: "Everyone has his own specific vocation or mission in life; everyone must carry out a concrete assignment that demands fulfillment."[1]

One of my go-to examples in talking to leaders about Purpose is the case of a highly intelligent, motivated undergrad who works tirelessly to get an aeronautical engineering degree at the University of North Dakota. On graduation, she can go to Boeing, to work on planes whose basic design hasn't changed in 50 years, or she can work for SpaceX, sending people to the stars and one day, perhaps colonizing Mars. Which will she choose? Which of these options is likely to attract the best and brightest, the top 1 percent of students, who can work wherever they want?

When that recent grad hears SpaceX's Purpose — *To make life multiplanetary* — and has a chance to help fulfill it, she hops in the car and drives all night to get to Texas. As parents, we ask: *What's the compensation? How many vacation days? Health benefits?* The answer from that graduate is: *I don't know or care — I'm going to change the world!*

This is the power of Purpose. Your organizational reason for existing does not have to be as adventurous as SpaceX's or as altruistic as Toms Shoes' to inspire workers, but it must be meaningful. Your business doesn't have to be as big as SpaceX

---

1   Viktor E. Frankl, *Man's Search for Meaning* (Beacon Press, 1959), 113.

either, to have a great Purpose. Fifty employees or a dozen —
as long as your Purpose is authentic, payroll isn't a factor.
Whatever you do, whatever your size, team members should
feel like they're on a "mission" with you, as Viktor Frankl put it,
doing important work that helps People in some way.

No one has written better about the power great companies
draw from Purpose than Simon Sinek. His seminal book *Start
with Why: How Great Leaders Inspire Everyone to Take Action,* and
his famous TED talk from 2009 used what he calls "the golden
circle" to explain Purpose. If you haven't seen this diagram,
picture concentric rings, as on a dartboard, with "why" in the
center, "how" encircling it, and "what" ringing the outer edge.

**SCAN TO
WATCH VIDEO**

Most companies, Sinek argues, work from the outside in. We all
know *what* we do — *we make quality widgets* — so we start with
that outer ring in our thoughts, communications, and actions.
Some companies know *how* they do it. The differentiating value
proposition or USP might be: *Our widgets are the most durable.*
Very few businesses, however, truly know *why* they do what

they do. When asked why they make widgets, the answer often involves money, but profit is a result, not a reason.

It's worth considering Sinek's example of Apple here, a company whose success many of us would love to emulate. If Apple operated like most businesses, its starting point would be: *We make great computers,* the "what" in the equation. They would then move to the "how" — *they're beautifully designed and simple to use* — before asking customers to buy them (note that, in typical fashion, no "why" gets mentioned).

Instead, Apple does the opposite, Sinek says, and starts with *why*:

1. **Why:** In everything we do, we believe in challenging the status quo and thinking differently.

2. **How:** We challenge the status quo by designing beautiful, user-friendly products.

3. **What:** We happen to make great computers, want to buy one?

This is the order that Sinek argues great leaders and organizations have always followed. If you're old enough to remember Apple's many famous ad campaigns, the company's marketing has always started with its *why*, from the "Think different" ads of the late '90s, featuring some of history's great disrupters (Einstein, King, Gandhi), to the 1984 riff on George Orwell's novel, *1984,* featuring a lone heroine in color (presumably, Apple personified), who awakens the gray dystopian masses to defy authority and break the stultifying status quo.

The Apple example highlights that Purpose is both inward- and outward-facing. It can engage and excite customers, partners, and vendors, as well as team members. If your *why* is strong, it won't stay locked in the building but will permeate sales, marketing, products, and services, inspiring your public, too. Apple sells an incredible range of products and services because its *why* has built intense trust and loyalty. People feel in their gut that this is a company which knows what they need before they do. As a business, that's an incredible place to live.

My advice is to also work from the inside out in developing and utilizing Purpose. It all starts with People, as I will ever shout from the mountaintops, and job one is finding the A-players who embrace your Purpose and values.

"The goal is not just to hire people who need a job, it's to hire people who believe what you believe," Sinek said in his now famous TED talk. "I always say, if you hire people who need a job, they'll work for your money, but if you hire people who believe what you believe, they'll work for you with their blood and sweat and tears."[2]

CULTURE

Inside the business, Purpose becomes the foundation of the complex amalgam we call "culture." That broad category includes your core values (whether you've articulated them or not) and other beliefs, your behaviors, actions, attitudes, and general M.O. Anytime you think, *this is how we do things around here* or *we're known for...*you're touching culture. You can think of it as your company's personality and as with people, it's the

2   Simon Sinek, "Start with Why: How Great Leaders Inspire Action," TEDx Talks, Sept. 29, 2009, YouTube video, https://youtu.be/u4ZoJKF_VuA.

thing that differentiates us and makes us who we are as an organization.

Apple, as we've seen, is a great example of how Purpose can build culture and set a business apart from the competition. Simon Sinek points out that other computer companies started with essentially the same basic tools, technology, and access as Apple, but in its Purpose, Apple had a great differentiator. That Purpose, the imperative to think differently and challenge the status quo, became the foundation for a unique culture that built trust and loyalty among customers and team members alike.

The opposite can also occur: a weak foundation leads to a weak structure. Countless companies with significant advantages — talented people, good products, strong capitalization, etc. — have been undercut by a lack of Purpose and poor culture. The impact of this gap can run the gamut, from a failure to thrive to anemic sales to complete failure.

I don't want to pick on Wells Fargo, and I hope its corporate culture has been cleaned up, but the bank's infamous scandal of a decade ago was the result of a Purposeless, toxic culture. The closest thing to a Purpose at Wells Fargo in the 2010s seems to have been a desire to make money on the backs of customers at all costs. Wildly unrealistic quotas and pressure tactics resulted in the creation of millions of fraudulent accounts, unwarranted fees, and other abuses. The first response from "leaders" as problems came to light was to blame individual workers and branch managers, but like all cultural problems, this one started at the top.

One way to think of Purpose and the culture that grows from it is to ask yourself what story you are telling the world. In the years before the 2008 financial crisis, Wells Fargo had taken comparatively few big risks and told the story of a stable, con-servative institution with a long history, commanding respect.

The dramatic shift in the story it told the world provides an important caveat: establishing Purpose is not a one-and-done exercise. Nurture it, and Purpose will pull you toward the peaks like a magic towrope. Neglect it, and weight grows throughout the organization until soon, you're dragging an anchor up the mountainside.

The story you tell the world — meaning People in and out of the organization — should differentiate you from the competition. This is the point of Purpose — to inspire with your unique, authentic mission, no matter how small your team or how narrow your niche.

My client, Discover Strength, doesn't operate on the scale of LA Fitness or Gold's Gym, but I would put its Purpose, culture, and unique story up against any. CEO Luke Carlson studied kinesiology and exercise physiology and was passionate about fitness from his student days. The more he learned, though, the more he realized that some of the most popular exercise regimens in the U.S. have no scientific basis whatsoever. Not only are many of them unproven, the programs encouraging 60-year-olds to jump on small boxes and hurl tires and barbells around, are often unsafe.

In response, Carlson founded Discover Strength, with the Purpose of *Leading the movement of evidence-based exercise.* This is why he gets out of bed in the morning, a reason that's authentic and inspiring — and differentiates Discover Strength from the competition. Everything the company does to help people improve health and fitness is based on science and evidence.

Who does this incredible Purpose attract? Believers, of course. In an industry where many trainers have no training (how's that for irony?), Luke's crew of certified exercise physiologists have four-year degrees in exercise science and are obsessed with strength training. His leadership team is, without a doubt, the fittest I've ever worked with (inspiring, yes, but I avoid mirrors and dessert for days after our meetings). These leaders all have their own training regimens, and they're as passionate about exercise as they are about driving the movement to base it on hard science. They don't just read the latest research in the field, they do their own — writing white papers, publishing studies, doing podcasts, and so on. As I've said, with believers like these on your leadership team, you can run up the mountain.

Discovering and articulating your Purpose can be a challenge, although, like core values, it's usually buried within that block of marble, ready to emerge with enough chipping away. Once it's expressed, figuring out how to deliver your Purpose and how it differentiates you in the course of doing business can be equally challenging. I don't want to give the impression that once you've stated a Purpose, the heavy lifting is done.

Bank Midwest, an institution based in Iowa, with branches in Iowa, South Dakota, and Minnesota, is a good example of a business continually working to deliver on its *why*. The bank's Purpose is simply: *To make lives better.* This team serves many small communities and are experts on helping the family farm, the new small business, kids heading off to college, or a couple buying a first home. When leaders began talking about developing an app to originate mortgages online and about lowering mortgage rates to compete with bigger rivals, I brought everyone back to Purpose.

Rocket Mortgage, a tech company in our space, will spend $250 million on their platform this year, I told the Bank Midwest team, and a consumer can get pre-approved there in 15 minutes. We can't compete with that, and we can't compete on rates with US Bank and Bank of America. You exist *To make lives better* in your communities, and you've told me that you nurture relationships that stand the test of time. You deliver on Purpose and differentiate yourself by knowing something about the family on that farm that needs a loan for a new tractor. You've served them for decades and know all about grandpa, who passed the land down, and Suzy, who's heading off to school, the price of corn, and the damage done by that last drought. You set yourself apart and fulfill your mission not with an app, but by showing up at the kitchen table, having a great conversation, and helping a family fill out an application.

Bank Midwest came to understand something I often tell clients — your Purpose helps you climb because it makes you special, not necessarily number one. Michael Porter, the father of modern strategy, said it well: "Strategy is about setting yourself apart from the competition. It's not a matter of being better at what you do — it's a matter of being different at what you do."[3]

ARTICULATE YOUR PURPOSE

Few parts of my job are more fun or challenging than helping leadership teams express the core Purpose that sets them apart. Sometimes it comes quickly. Usually, it takes serious effort and many passes, much hand-wringing and tweaking of language, before we get it right. There is no substitute, in my opinion, for involving an outside set of eyes in this process, preferably ones that have seen many businesses inside and out — and are connected to a brain that knows something about Purpose.

---

3   Michael Porter. AZQuotes.com, Wind and Fly LTD, 2025. https://www. AZQuotes.com/quote/871412, accessed April 04, 2025.

Remember the adage, "We don't know who discovered water, but we know it wasn't the fish." Leaders must create their own Purpose statements, of course, but they are the fish in this scenario. They're often surprisingly blind to things they do well or care deeply about because those elements are so engrained in them and in the business. If you undertake the effort to state your Purpose without a Guide, bounce your results off trusted, experienced leaders from outside the company for the non-piscine view.

I usually begin our core Purpose journey at Base Camp by presenting to leaders five fundamentals of a good Purpose statement. We've already discussed these concepts, so I'll just list them briefly:

- **Inspiring.** Your Purpose must be inspiring for team members and help them find meaning in their work.

- **Lasting.** A good Purpose is timeless, as valid in 100 years as it is today. While a company might have several Pinnacles over the years, it usually has one Purpose.

- **Expansive.** Your Purpose should help you think expansively about what you *could* be doing but aren't. Think big!

- **Focusing.** A good Purpose helps you decide what to do and equally important, what not to do.

- **Authentic.** Your expression of what you stand for must be true to who you are as an organization. Companies that fail on this count often don't stand for anything.

You want every team member to know your Purpose as well as they know their names. To this end, keep it simple and clear, one or two sentences max — preferably, one. Simple does not mean flat or dull, though dull is better than too fancy or overly complex. You don't want a glib or superficial statement and meaning has primacy, but catchy, lyrical, even poetic, isn't a bad thing. Pella WYIDAHO's Purpose, *To create a river of raving fans who flourish in life,* is authentic and inspiring, and on a pure language level, the alliteration — that repetition of R and F sounds — is a nice touch. It makes the Purpose memorable, and a dash of poetry — as long as it's backed by action — can be inspiring in its own right.

To give leaders a feel for what a good Purpose looks like, I always present some examples from well-known companies:

 **Tesla:** To accelerate the world's transition to sustainable energy.

 **Lego:** To inspire and develop the builders of tomorrow.

 **Whole Foods.** To nourish people and the planet.

 **BMW.** To enable people to experience the joy of driving.

 **Microsoft.** To empower every person and every organization on the planet to achieve more.

So that everyone understands giant corporations aren't the only ones with great Purposes, I give leaders some examples from Pinnacle Business Guides clients too:

 **Pella Northland:** To improve people's view of the world and their place in it.

 **Pella WYIDAHO:** To create a river of raving fans who flourish in life.

 **Acucraft:** To make a positive impact.

 **Comstock Construction:** Building on our legacy of people helping people (Comstock is 100 years old).

 **Hempel Companies:** To create better lives for those we serve.

 **Dempsey Construction:** To build a company filled with inspired, exceptional people.

 **Media Minefield:** To unlock the power in stories to positively impact lives!

 **Coordinated Business Systems:** To unleash the power of people.

 **The Union Bank & Trust:** To be a safe harbor for union finances.

I then work through the Core Purpose worksheet, a Pinnacle tool which asks leaders, quite simply, "Why do we exist?" (to make the world a better place)? There is space to work on the question and then more space to edit and revise the initial drafts into something polished. That worksheet is accompanied by a Purpose test, which you will find below. Leaders answer the test questions individually to gauge their reaction to a proposed Purpose statement. Most People in the group, ideally two-thirds or more, must answer "yes" to all the questions for the Purpose to be a keeper. Fewer than that, and it's back to the drawing board.

CORE PURPOSE TEST: IS IT THE REAL DEAL?

Let's see if our new Core Purpose truly inspires and guides us.

INSTRUCTIONS:

- Take a few quiet minutes on your own.

- Reflect on the six questions below.

- Answer honestly. If most of the team can't confidently say **YES** to *all six*, we're not done yet. Keep refining until at least two-thirds of us are fully aligned.

CORE
PURPOSE
TEST
QUESTIONS

1 Does this purpose genuinely inspire me?

2 Does it open up exciting, long-term possibilities for our future—far beyond what we do today?

3 Does it help us clearly say *no* to things that don't fit?

4 Does it feel real—something we actually believe and live out, not just nice words?

5 Would most people here feel energized and excited by it (not cynical)?

6 If I told my kids or loved ones about this purpose, would I feel proud?

NEXT STEP:
If you answered **YES** to all six, great—we're on the right track! If not, let's talk and refine together.

USE (OR LOSE) YOUR *WHY*

Often, leadership teams I work with already have some version of a written Purpose, or mission statement, and core values. I always applaud those efforts, which show their heads and hearts are in the right place. It can be an embarrassing moment, though, when I ask a couple random leaders to state the company's Purpose and core values. Some garble the Purpose, misstating it, or they can only limp through two of the five core values. Frequently, phones come out, as the COO and CFO scramble to check the company website for an answer.

HINT: IF YOU HAVE TO CHECK A WEBSITE FOR YOUR PURPOSE, YOU DON'T HAVE ONE.

In all seriousness, time is precious, executives are busy. Why waste hours getting leaders to articulate a Purpose if a month later, no one remembers it? You might as well gather to play Wordle, which at least offers a relaxing break from the stress of running a business.

There's nothing easy or relaxing about a Purpose initiative, so if you're going to bother, it should at the very least pass what I call the 3 a.m. test. If I call any of our Pinnacle team members at 3 a.m. and ask after that groggy, alarmed hello, they should be able to instantly rattle off our Purpose. I want our team members to wake up in the morning thinking, *How am I going to positively impact lives, one client and one mountain at a time today?* And at night, I want them to doze off thinking, as I do, *How did I positively impact lives today? Which clients did I help? Which mountains did we climb?*

If leaders don't remember your Purpose, you might have the wrong one. It could be either so uninspiring or so inauthentic that no one takes it seriously. If that's the case, remedies range from making minor revisions to creating something completely new. See the section above on how to articulate a better Purpose that's true to who you really are as an organization.

If after soul searching, though, you believe that you have the right Purpose and it's still ignored, the problem is that *you* are not taking it seriously. Purpose, as I've said, is not one-and-done, a box to be checked, or a hollow exercise you perform because all the cool kids are doing it. Your *why* has to be exactly that — the reason you exist, the thing that gets you out of bed in the morning — and to be effective, it must be incorporated into every layer of the organization — hiring, employee reviews, marketing, sales, strategy...

Does this take work? You bet it does. It takes serious effort and buy-in from leaders, managers, and supervisors throughout the organization. As I hope I've argued effectively, though, a solid Purpose and Pinnacle goal eventually will save far more work than they require, as team members at all levels realize they have a compass to aid in decision-making. They'll have more autonomy and as they embark on an epic journey, will feel inspired and aligned, fulfilling a Purpose that helps people.

I've touched on a variety of ways to embed Purpose and a Pinnacle goal into your business, but here's a quick overview.

- **Socialization.** This is low-hanging fruit and a good way to get started. Socialize your Purpose and Pinnacle by posting them at the reception desk, the lunchroom, and elsewhere on site. Get your Purpose on the walls, into Playbooks, and in team member materials.

- **Strategy.** Purpose is your compass. Let it guide your goals, milestones, rocks, etc. It must be part of the Vision Statement, annual state of the company messaging, and all strategy documents.

- **Meetings.** Meetings are miserable, at least for many companies, because they're desultory and direction-less. Gain direction by making Purpose and your Pinnacle a part of all meetings. For example, at Doug Phelps' shop, managers ask in weekly team meetings, "How did you deliver E3 (the company's Pinnacle) this week?"

- **Hiring**. Use Purpose in recruiting and hiring to attract A-players who believe and to repel the People who don't.

- **Training**. Make your Purpose and Pinnacle part of training and onboarding, connecting them to concrete policies and procedures.

- **Employee Reviews**. How did each team member deliver on Purpose and move us closer to our Pinnacle goal? This question should be a part of every quarterly conversation.

- **Marketing, Products.** Purpose starts in-house, but as we saw with Apple, it's also a part of your brand and a great differentiator for customers. How are you delivering on Purpose through products, services, marketing, etc.?

A strong Purpose is vital for team health, aligning and inspiring People at all levels. But your *why* is useless without a strong *how*. In our next chapter, on Playbooks, we'll explore how Purpose becomes process, using Playbooks to systemize and optimize the business, so that leaders can focus on the climb.

MOUNTAIN LOOKBACK

- **Purpose Builds Meaning.** An authentic Purpose captures what you stand for and who you are and answers the question, *where are we headed?*

- **Articulate a Purpose.** Your Purpose should be permanent, aspirational, inspiring, and authentic. Good ones mention helping people or making the world better — never money.

- **A Compass**. Purpose gives your team direction, orienting everyone. It is strategic, helping you decide not just where you're going but how to get there.

- **Competitive Advantage**. A powerful Purpose sets you apart from the competition, building trust and loyalty among customers and team members.

- **Pinnacle Goal.** Your "Pinnacle" is a major goal worthy of the climb, usually with a 5 to 7-year timeframe. You have one Purpose but might have several Pinnacles over years.

- **A Filter**. Purpose becomes a decision-making filter for the whole team, a way to test which choices align with our climb.

- **Embed Purpose.** Use your Purpose in hiring, training, and reviewing team members. Socialize it. Place it on signs, cups, web pages, etc. — and at the heart of every meeting.

- **Purposeful Hiring**. Interview to determine if prospective hires align with your Purpose, Pinnacle, and core values, not just to assess their skills.

- **Inspiration**. We all want meaning and a mission in our lives. "Start with *why*," as Simon Sinek says, to inspire and motivate team members.

CHAPTER 4

PLAYBOOKS

BECOME A SYSTEMS-BASED BUSINESS

His fellow professionals in the health club space regularly ask David Gschneidner, Vice President of Operations at Discover Strength, how the company gets such exceptional people at its locations' — young workers who greet clients warmly, are never on their phones, and communicate effectively.

"The interpersonal skills that they use are all in our Playbook for delivering world-class customer service," David says. "It's part of a documented process they get the very first day that they're with us. They practice professional greetings. We tell them to smile, aim your smile, shake hands like you mean it, continue the conversation. We never have our phones on the floor. Those get put in the back office, and so it's literally never been an issue for us."

The "Playbook" David mentions is the Pinnacle Business Guides tool for documenting every important, repeatable process in a business. Playbooks are simple in a way. You might think of them as checklists that document the various processes that make your business run. How do we onboard a client, review a vendor contract, enter payments in accounts receivable, train a new hire? These and other processes get analyzed, streamlined, and documented in Playbooks, which regulate the organization, improving everything from management to marketing to sales.

Playbooks is the third of our five fundamental principles for business success and lives at the pivotal point in the middle, with People on one end and Profit on the other. Like a fulcrum, Playbooks can leverage People and Purpose into Performance and Profit by helping you to analyze, optimize, and document the things you already do every day.

Simple, right? Sure, but for most businesses, simplicity isn't so simple, which is why many either never get around to documenting repeatable, scalable processes in something like a Playbook — or don't do a good job of creating and maintaining them long-term.

Neglect of this sort was never an option for Discover Strength. The company's Purpose, as I mentioned in the previous chapter, is *To lead the movement of evidence-based exercise,* and its Pinnacle goal is *To become THE destination for resistance exercise as medicine* over the next decade. As I write this,

Discover Strength has 51 locations, which stretch from Utah to Georgia, and to reach its Pinnacle, it hopes to have five times as many — 250 total — by 2035.

Growth is difficult and franchising is impossible without Playbooks, but David says they would be "wildly important" even if Discover Strength had only a single location.

"One of our unique value propositions is that you're working with an educated, expert exercise professional with a four-year degree," he says. "We have a shared-client model, so at one location, myself and six other staff are working with all our clients. We have to be uniform in delivery of the workout, while also understanding that each of us is going to be different inter-personally. We don't want robots, but we can't have what we would call experience roulette."

Having worked with Discover Strength for around a decade, it's impossible for me to point to any one element of the business as the key to its success (they do too many things too well), but I can say with certainty that the company's embrace of Playbooks helps create an exemplary experience not only for clients, but also for employees and managers.

Discover Strength has Playbooks for the broad categories present at most businesses — marketing, sales, manage-ment, meetings, financials, etc. According to David, some of the key "plays," the individual processes within the Playbooks, document how to deliver the workout, perform as a manager, and be a great exercise practitioner. I'll return to his examples later, but for now, I want to point out that at Discover Strength, Playbooks are key to having the business run like a machine (giving leaders time to focus on growth) and to delivering the worldclass customer experience at the heart of the brand.

Descriptors like "worldclass" get tossed around lightly, so I'll put that claim in perspective by noting that a Net Promotor

Score (NPS) over 50 is generally considered excellent, and Discover Strength's is well in the 90s. Business Strategist, Fred Reichheld, introduced the NPS in a 2003 *Harvard Business Review* article titled "The One Number You Need to Grow," arguing that it's the best predictor of return business and word-of-mouth promotion. The NPS is a fantastic predictor of growth — and an extremely tough metric — because it doesn't just measure customer satisfaction or even loyalty but the likelihood that consumers will take that additional, proactive step of recommending a product or service to others. A stellar NPS demands not just an incredible customer experience but an incredibly consistent one. Such consistency, as Discover Strength leaders know, is possible only with well-integrated Playbooks.

"We have this stuff built into our meeting cadence, which allows us to bring the plays back up, remind everyone about them, practice them, role-play them..." David says. "We need to make sure that our Playbooks are alive in the business and not just on a sheet of paper because they have allowed us to have significantly better customer service and are largely the reason why we have the NPS that we have."

WHY SMALL COMPANIES STAY SMALL

This chapter is the one that can make you love your life again. It's the one that can give you back evenings and weekends, lower your blood pressure, and reintroduce you to your spouse and kids.

That's no exaggeration.

I have worked with thousands of entrepreneurs over decades, and their biggest source of daily pain usually involves our third principle, Playbooks, or I should say, a lack of Playbooks. The pain of People, which I discussed in Chapter 2, is devastating, but People can be let go, hired, changed. The pain of Process is chronic. You can get the best People in the world, have a strong Purpose and unifying Pinnacle goal, but if you don't have systems in place, solid repeatable processes that are documented and ingrained, the daily headaches, fresh fires — insert your favorite cliché for problems here — will not diminish.

In fact, those quality People, the A-players you treasure, can slip into B and even C terrain when faced with a flurry of ad-hoc processes that are inefficient or inadequate, or which change depending on who's in charge. We addressed the *who* of your business in Chapter 2, on People, and the *why* in Chapter 3, on Purpose. Here, we are addressing the *what*, the utterly concrete, practical things you do to succeed every day. I don't call Playbooks the *how*, as some might, because at Pinnacle, the model isn't granular or overly prescriptive. As I'll explain later, these are not detailed SOPs (standard operating procedures), policies, or manuals, but checklists, providing a simple, skeletal view of every important process in the business.

We call our depositories of process "Playbooks" because, as with the detailed plays designed by sports teams, they should be at the heart of our strategy and a source of great competitive advantage. Can you imagine an NFL team hitting the gridiron on a Sunday without a detailed Playbook that coaches and players sweated over, refined, and internalized? They would just as soon take to the field naked. Any day of the week, I would put my money on a college team with a good Playbook competing against a pro team without one. The college team with well-considered plays maximizes its People for Performance, getting the absolute most out of them (and keeping them happy), while the hypothetical pro team without a Playbook wastes its People and their talents (and frustrates A-players who will take their annoyance out on each other).

The sports analogy built into Playbooks highlights just how valuable the codification of process is. When a storied football coach like Bill Belichick finds himself at fourth and long, third and goal, or whatever the situation, everything depends on that list of clear, practiced plays he knows his team can execute in that moment. Without them, he's nothing as a coach, and his talented players are individual athletes, not a team. Belichick's most coveted tool and stock-in-trade is his Playbook, and like other good coaches he wouldn't part with it for a million dollars.

If you don't have Playbooks as a leader, you don't have a way to execute efficiently, which means that whatever plan you think you have is toothless. As the old quote often attributed to Thomas Edison has it, "Ideas without execution are hallucinations." Playbooks give you the means to execute, to realize your ideas.

Purpose is your compass as you lead People up the mountain toward your Pinnacle. Playbooks are the map, or a series of maps, showing every team member how to get through the key segments of the journey. If our navigator gets sick and returns to Base Camp, we still know where we're climbing to and what we must do to get there. The expedition rolls on. If three team members leave, their replacements hit the ground running, with clear instructions. Like a machine with unstoppable momentum, the expedition rolls on.

Without Playbooks, the expedition moves in fits and starts. We don't operate as a team, with clear expectations and coordinated maps to reference. The smallest bump in the road can stall our expedition on the mountainside, and the loss of our leader, or navigator, who has the only Playbook locked in his head, can halt it for good.

An absence of Playbooks is the top reason why small businesses stay small — and why entrepreneurs have ulcers. Such businesses run on tribal knowledge, which exists in the brain of the owner or CEO. Performance and the customer experience vary widely, since there isn't one documented process for all the stuff we do. How we handle new customers depends on whether Ben, the owner, is in that day, or Ryan, his second in command. Employee training is very different in the hands of Ben, who leaves big gaps, than in the hands of Leslie, a notorious micromanager. There isn't one process for accounts payable but three — one for each person in that department.

Leaders are constantly sucked into such a business, consumed with minutiae and fires that need dousing. They don't have time to envision their Pinnacle, much less make a plan to get there. Whether or not we recognize this dynamic in our own businesses, we encounter it in others all the time, right? I'll only eat at Julie's Cafe on the weekends, when Julie herself cooks, because the weekday guy sucks. Steve is the only mechanic at that shop who can fix my car, so if he's on vacation, I'll go to the dealer. I can't see any dentist in the practice besides Dr. Gregory. The others don't understand pain management... Without Playbooks, Ben, Julie, and Dr. Gregory are too mired in performing basic processes and fixing mistakes to work on the business.

Organizations like these, even with great People and strong Purpose, will forever be stuck in the foothills unless they commit to documenting the repeatable, scalable processes they run on. Employee performance will remain uneven, and their customers will forever play "experience roulette," as David Gschneidner puts it.

That all changes — in fact, everything changes — once you commit to Playbooks.

The big difference between McDonald's and your business is Playbooks. That's it. They make hamburgers, for crying out loud, and no offense — this comes from a great admirer of the company's commercial prowess — the burgers are not especially good. What they are, in spades, is consistent. Whether you order a Big Mac, a Filet-O-Fish, or a vanilla shake, it'll be the same in South Bend and Seattle, Dublin or Dubai. The process for cooking your Quarter Pounder has been analyzed intensely, tweaked until perfect, and then codified for cooks in 40,000 locations serving nearly 70 million people each day. In Portland, Maine and in San Diego, California tomorrow McDonald's employees will put the same amount of seasoning on a beef patty that will be seared and cooked on one side for the same amount of time before being turned and cooked on the other for the same amount of time, then placed on a bun with the same fixings stacked in the same order. Employees will be trained and promoted based on the same practices at each of those locations, ingredients will be ordered and tracked in the same way, and bills will be paid using the same systems.

Companies like McDonald's and Starbucks are masters of Playbooks. This, more than anything, is what got them to the highest peaks. There is no other way to scale your business or get to your Pinnacle goal. Pinnacles demand carefully considered, documented processes, but even if you don't intend to grow, consider how much better your life would be if your business operated like a machine. Imagine leading a company where everyone, from the receptionist to the CFO, had a set of plays documenting every important, repeatable process they touched. Imagine yourself and other leaders being asked half as many questions in an average day. Imagine training for new employees that is half as difficult and twice as effective. Imagine your team members, products, and services consistent at all times and locations, boosting the customer experience.

Most of all, imagine cutting down on the fires and daily minutiae, so that you have more time to think about the big picture, to weigh opportunities and threats, to build strategies that really go after the competition. Imagine more time to vacation, hang with the family, golf, fish, or whatever you're into, knowing that your business can manage itself while you're gone.

Wasn't that always the dream? It is for most budding entrepreneurs, but the day never comes. In a horribly circular argument, they say they don't have the time or energy for documenting the key processes — the thing that gives them more time.

Luckily, creating Playbooks doesn't take much of either. As I'll explore in this chapter, the effort of creating and maintaining Playbooks can be spread across the team. New software and AI make the kinds of checklists we're talking about easier than ever to build. You don't need to devote a staff person to this. The cost is hard to measure because it's so small, and the ROI is immeasurable because it's so big.

WHY PLAYBOOKS?

Every good business operating system has some way of documenting the core processes a business runs on. This is one of the chief benefits of using an operating system — gaining the means to systemize, optimize, and document business functions. Such an initiative works best with an expert Guide to advise leaders, I think, and hold feet to the fire when necessary, but the only requirement is a commitment to optimize and document your processes.

Before we get into making Playbooks, I'll spend a moment on exactly what they are and, equally important, are not. Leaders sometimes tell me that they don't need Playbooks because they already have detailed training manuals and a full set of SOPs. I am always glad to hear they have these tools — it demonstrates the right mindset — but those are not Playbooks.

SOPs and training manuals are like *The Oxford English Dictionary* of business process. They are terrific if you're after every nuance and arcane implication of a task, but People quickly drown in all that info. SOPs and training manuals delve deep into the Purpose, scope, and responsibilities of each process, with too many steps to be useful. They are granular and highly prescriptive and for that reason, more likely to cause paralysis than clarity for a worker looking for a point of reference.

Some also mistake policies for Playbooks. Policies provide the guidelines we follow in specific situations but they're at the other end of the spectrum from SOPs. They often contain minimal or no helpful steps to complete a process. *We don't take returns after 30 days.* This is a policy. What happens when an irate customer shows up, wanting to return something after 34 days? The policy is vague at best on this question, while the SOP or training manual might devote three detailed pages to it.

The pertinent play in your customer Playbook aims for the sweet spot between these two — a simple checklist with maybe six or 10 steps, giving an overview of how we handle the situation.

To return to our sports analogy, for a 15-yard slant, the "play" is: run 15 yards straight out, then break sharply at a 45-degree angle to cut across the middle of the field. The SOP and training manual entries here would tell the player, keep your left foot forward, toes one inch behind the line, hunch to lower your center of gravity, take 11 steps forward after the snap, then planting your left foot firmly, pivot with your right to change to a 45 to 60-degree trajectory...etc. The policy might simply state that a slant is one of the effective plays we can use against a blitz.

As I hope you can see from these examples, the internalized skeletal checklist is invaluable for the player on the field. It's basic enough to remember clearly, and it grants them autonomy. We're not saying how to place your foot at the line or how to hold the ball, just outlining the broad steps you should follow.

Fine, but can a "checklist" this basic be effective? I'm asked this by leaders convinced that their processes are too complex for such a simple tool. In reply, I point out that checklists are used every day to perform surgery and build skyscrapers. Surely, your tasks aren't more complex than those?

The surgery example reminds me of a meeting one of our Pinnacle Business Guides had with a dentist who was sure that his complex procedures could never be written as checklists.

"You might be right," the Guide said, "But humor me. What's your first procedure tomorrow?"

The dentist said he was doing an endodontic retreatment first thing — essentially, a double root canal. The Guide grabbed his tablet and typed into AI, "Best practices for an endodontic retreatment." A checklist immediately appeared. The dentist read it and looked up, astonished.

"That is the exact protocol I follow," he said. "It's what I'll do tomorrow, every step."

No matter how complex we think our processes are, they can be simplified into the form of a basic play or checklist (surgery included). If a process truly can't be turned into a checklist, it's time to analyze it for streamlining and optimization. As theater legend David Belasco said, "If you can't write your idea on the back of my calling card, you don't have a clear idea."

MAKING YOUR PLAYBOOKS

It's never been easier, as I've noted, to document your processes in Playbooks, thanks in part to AI and helpful software (I'll introduce my favorite process software, Trainual, in a moment, and another for meetings, called Strety). You don't need to dedicate a team member to creating Playbooks. The payoff is enormous, the timeline quick, the expense zero to nominal, and the only requirement is a commitment from leadership to get it done.

My advice is to spread the effort across the organization. A typical company might have 10 to 15 Playbooks covering processes in all the categories you would expect: sales, marketing, operations, finance, technology, customer experience, etc. Each Playbook, of course, is made up of various plays, one for each of the important processes in that category. The New Customer Playbook, for instance, might have six or eight plays for onboarding a new customer.

The leadership team should take charge of Playbooks and own the process of creating them start to finish. Your CMO will own the Marketing Playbook, your COO the Operations Playbook, the Vice President of Sales your Sales and New Customer Playbooks, etc. "Owning" includes making sure that all key plays are documented and that the completed Playbooks are incorporated into daily operations, regularly maintained, continuously trained on, and updated. Leaders can assign individual plays to team members in relevant departments, so that every individual play also has an owner responsible for making sure it's used and updated.

How long does it take to create Playbooks for your whole organization?

How committed are you? Many companies that decide to thoroughly document their processes never complete the project, or they create Playbooks but fail to integrate them into operations. They exist somewhere on a bookshelf or Google Drive but are not "alive in the business," as David Gschneidner, of Discover Strength, puts it. If you're not fully committed, or not ready yet, don't bother. Why waste precious time?

If you are committed, you can have Playbooks assigned to the leaders who will own them next week and a full set — at least, a first pass at a full set — comfortably completed within one quarter. A typical rhythm for my clients is: one quarter for creation, one quarter for rollout, and one quarter for a refresh. Playbooks can be going full-force, running your business like a self-propelled machine and freeing up your time within a year.

There are three ways to begin a Playbooks initiative.

- **Scavenger Hunt**. Collect everything you have, every shred of each process, all instructions, policies, SOPs, and process memos as the raw material for Playbooks. Companies using this method will find that they have half a dozen versions of many processes, highlighting the need for a single, optimized Playbook. Simplify and organize this material into plays, revise them, test them, and assemble Playbooks.

- **Mature Model**. Use one mature business process at your company to serve as a paradigm. Optimize it, test it, revise it, then distribute it to leaders to use as a model as they build Playbooks.

- **New template.** Choose an important process and start from scratch to create a brand-new play, optimizing and then documenting it. Distribute it to leaders to use as a template for the Playbooks they're in charge of.

Each play should begin by stating its goal, and all must be concise. If a play doesn't fit on a single page, it's too long — you've strayed into SOP territory. One painless, even fun possibility for composing your plays is to gather the team that performs a particular process. The leader in charge distributes Post-it notes and asks everyone to write down every step. Ask for a volunteer to post step one on the wall, then discuss. Almost always, this person has missed the actual first step — they write about the quarterback throwing the ball rather than the snap or lineup. Have someone else try until we have the real step one, then polish it until we agree it's perfect.

DOCUMENTING
THE
WHAT
NOT HOW.

Do the same with subsequent steps, discussing each as you go. Usually, you end up with far too many steps, and 50 must be boiled down to the six or eight essential parts of the process. Steps should be as simple as possible and few as possible without shortchanging the process. Writing three pages — the SOP — is easy. Creating a concise checklist of six critical items is tough. Someone once famously apologized for sending a long letter, noting that he didn't have enough time to write a short one. This is the crux of creating plays.

Once a play is drafted, you obviously need to test it. Watch it performed, solicit feedback from those performing it, and analyze results. Did we get it right? What's missing? What's superfluous? How can we tweak this process to make it more efficient and effective? Revise until you feel it's ready to add to the Playbook, realizing that all plays will evolve and be updated at some point, as circumstances change or we think of improvements.

As you complete Playbooks, come up with a consistent naming convention, preferably one that reflects your business and its core values. If one of your core values is to be the "secret sauce" that helps your clients build mighty brands, your Sales Playbook might be called "Secret Sales Sauce," your Ops Playbook "Secret Ops Sauce," etc. The Tao, Manifesto, Code... whatever suits, but make it fun and reflective of your culture.

I often recommend that clients begin this journey with two of the most important Playbooks — the Employee Experience Playbook and the Client Experience Playbook. Both deal with People, and as you know by now, we're all in the People business. These two Playbooks involve many, if not all, departments, and both are vitally important to your climb. If you get these ones right, you will have improved systems across the organization and will be energized to create more.

LIVING PLAYBOOKS

Once Playbooks are complete — ideally, before then — we need a place to keep them. They must be accessible, easily updated, and incorporated into the fabric of the business — living things — or they die. If you doubt the importance of this utilitarian concern, ask your nearest team member where you can find the company training manual and when they last used it. Both questions are probably tough to answer. This is one reason we use Playbooks daily to systemize processes and not that intimidating tome of SOPs or the training manual that resembles an encyclopedia.

A company called Trainual, a Preferred Partner of Pinnacle Business Guides, helps you to document processes in a digital system that's accessible to all and easily updated. The editing interface makes it simple to document a process from scratch and then embed videos, GIFs, PDFs, etc. to enhance each play. If you already have documentation, you can upload it into your digital playbooks, whatever the format — PDF, Word, MP3, etc. Trainual has more than 400 industry-proven templates you can browse and then customize for your business (perhaps discovering along the way steps from others that you'll want to add to your process).

One of the more exciting and time-saving features of Trainual is that you can also choose to have processes document themselves. The platform's built-in AI capabilities allow you to enter a process and parameters, and it will instantly write the play for you. Customize the AI creation for your business, and a play can be done in minutes.

I don't have space here to delve into Trainual's many capabilities, everything from creating custom quizzes on plays for team members to connecting Playbooks to People and assigning training paths for great onboarding experiences. I was instantly smitten with Trainual because it addresses one of the biggest problems with documented processes — even good documentation winds up moldering in some storage closet. With Trainual, utility, integration, easy access, and regular updates are built in.

Strety, another Pinnacle Preferred Partner, does for meetings what Trainual does for Playbooks. Meetings are vitally important, yet almost universally hated because they lack direction and clear objectives. I mention Strety because its customized platform provides an ideal Playbook for your meetings. The software includes a digital agenda, which is connected to Rocks (our quarterly goals), our weekly scoreboard (more on this in Chapter 5), fresh issues, topics from the previous week's meeting, and a host of other interactive metrics and information.

Team members are frustrated by rambling meetings — all talk, scant results. Strety keeps meetings focused and connects the talk to action — or lack of action — which everyone can follow onscreen. Did we "Win the week?" Are our priorities on track? Who needs to know what, moving forward? Who addressed or failed to address last week's topics and how can we move them off this agenda and into the "done" column? With templated agendas, problems, causes, desired outcomes, and accountability are tracked, displayed, and synced with action items.

Meetings should be one of your greatest tools, your stage and place to shine, as I'll discuss in our next chapter. If they are subpar, something vital is broken. Strety is one of the best ways I know to fix it.

AUTONOMY AND EFFICIENCY

I've argued that Playbooks should be built into the fabric of your business, powering every department and each important process — onboarding, sales, training, meetings, you name it — until the company becomes a self-regulating machine, freeing up time for leaders to lead. But how do Playbooks work once they're in place and what are their concrete effects? If the company runs like a machine, is there a danger of treating People like so many gears, stifling creativity and autonomy?

I want to address these questions and paint a picture of life with Playbooks before we leave the third of our five fundamental principles.

First of all, Playbooks are consciously designed to avoid stifling creativity, dehumanizing team members, or eliminating autonomy. If one of your People is onboarding a new customer, do you want them to spend all their time and energy on the process, working to remember and perform various steps, or do you want the process to be second nature, so they can pay attention to the client and cultivate a genuine human connection? "Systemize the predictable so you can humanize the exceptional," said Isadore Sharp, founder of the Four Seasons — and unknowingly captured the soul of Playbooks. Simple checklists help us cover our predictable bases, so that we can focus on the higher-order elements of the business — exceptional human interactions, exceptional service, exceptional leadership.

Playbooks, as I've explained, are not prescriptive. They are the *what*, not the *how,* which means team members retain plenty of autonomy in how they get things done. If part of our employee onboarding process involves prepping and decorating the new hire's desk for her first day and then taking her on a facilities tour, it will be up to the person handling that process to decide what supplies they'll stock and how they'll decorate — *Flowers or balloons? Bought from where?* — and how to put together that tour of the building.

David Gschneidner, of Discover Strength, says that granting autonomy to the A-players his company recruits is just as important as having documented processes to guide them. Playbooks achieve both.

"We don't want to handcuff our exercise professional to say, this is the cookie-cutter way that you're going to do this," David says. "We want to kind of put those bumpers up and say, within these parameters, you have a ton of autonomy to deliver things based on the context you're in, injuries that that person has, their unique mentality, or whatever. This is really important because we're not going to retain our exercise physiologists if we're so prescriptive they have no autonomy in their work."

Team members not only retain autonomy with Playbooks, they have more space for creativity and self-determination as processes become smoother and more efficient. Entrepreneurs think of Playbooks as a way to document existing processes, but they also, inherently, call for analyzing and optimizing those processes, so the initiative itself is invaluable. However you go about documenting your plays — gathering teams for the Post-it method described above, assembling all existing materials to combine, or observing a process and writing a new play from scratch — you have to break the process down and distill its essence.

Throughout that journey, leaders and team members must eliminate multiple versions of how something gets done and consolidate the chaos into one optimal process. Once you con-solidate versions into a single play, the refinement and revision continue. You must ask, wait, is this step really necessary? Why are we doing this? Wouldn't this function be handled better in

Finance, as part of their Playbook? Steps 2 and 6 are repetitive, should they be combined?

We are constantly streamlining, eliminating, adding, testing, and revising. The process of making Playbooks leads not just to documented processes, but better processes — as well as better team members. A Playbooks initiative encourages the kind of systems-thinking you want not just from leaders but frontline workers, too. They are the ones frustrated by bottlenecks, roadblocks, duplication, and waste on the ground. They often have great suggestions for improving processes and systems, given a chance to express their ideas. Creating and updating Playbooks builds that chance into your business and gets team members invested in discovering the best ways to climb.

Workflows will become more efficient and effective as Playbooks are created because every important process gets analyzed in what amounts to a full systems-audit. Businesses inevitably realize there's a better, faster, or more affordable way to do things that have been yoked to laborious legacy processes. In addition to simple efficiencies, the new, improved process might enlist automation, touchless technology, AI, IoT (the Internet of things), or SaaS (software as a service). The idea isn't to replace People, though some processes might be taken over wholly or partly by technological solutions, but to free People to focus on the critical human elements of the business.

IMPROVE EXPECTATIONS, RETENTION

People work better and have greater job satisfaction when processes are clear and efficient. Just as Playbooks build cohesiveness on sports teams, they boost teamwork in businesses while establishing a kind of self-alignment. We know by the time Playbooks are in place who is doing what, who is responsible for every process, and how each process should be performed. There's no infighting about the best way to do something. That argument gets settled as you discuss each step, creating your plays. When a question does arise, we consult the Playbook. Theoretically, team members at companies with thick training manuals also have a handy reference to settle questions, but manuals and SOPs are so unwieldy, employees would rather wing it than consult them.

Playbooks don't just settle questions among frontline workers, cutting down on the number of queries managers have to field. They do the same for leaders, David Gschneidner says, providing everyone with "a source of truth."

"There are still fires when you have Playbooks, but what I think they do is provide clarity, so when a fire comes up, we have a source of truth to go back to," David says. "I don't want to memorize everything, and I don't want our business to rely on tribal knowledge, which so many organizations do — stuff that's passed down and doesn't live anywhere."

By way of example, David says he sometimes hears a leader at Discover Strength say something about how an exercise is done and thinks, I don't know if that's right. He consults the Workout Playbook, which has a checklist for every exercise, and reads the relevant play for an answer.

In addition to being a source of truth, Playbooks are a source of expectations, which is gold for leaders. So many problems in management arise from a lack of clear expectations, it's hard to overstate the value of having them set down clearly in Playbooks. Once your plays are in place, People should know exactly what's expected of them for every process they perform. Excuses diminish, and so does poor management.

I'm reminded of a client who was suffering 40 percent turnover in the company warehouse. At the time, I didn't say, but definitely thought, *What in hell is going on out there to create that kind of attrition?* The guy in charge was a drill sergeant type who subscribed to the doctrine of management by yelling. People weren't being trained or supervised well. The warehouse manager lacked the disposition to succeed, as well as the tools. Developing a full set of Playbooks for onboarding, training, and all warehouse processes dramatically improved the environment and made managing much easier for his replacement.

Park Chrysler Jeep, in Burnsville, MN, one of my star clients, provides another example of the power of Playbooks. They've worked so hard at hiring great People, I use the list that I helped Park Chrysler Jeep leaders create, "What A-Players Want," as an example for other companies (I'll print it in Chapter 5, on Performance). They care deeply about having a great team, but when I began as their Pinnacle Business Guide, 17 People had left just several months earlier.

The most important thing we did to boost retention was to create Playbooks. We needed to make improvements in how People were being trained, and the New Employee Playbook ensured that everyone was trained in the same way and learning the same key things — no gaps. Once they were onboard, the pertinent department Playbook — sales, finance, marketing, etc. — created clear expectations and helped them work through every process they touched with confidence.

Having plays to draw on set up team members for success — and made their managers better at managing. Their expectations were also clearer, their training skills sharper. A year later, Park Chrysler Jeep lost just one person in January, always a tough month for car sales. No one in business needs to spend much time calculating the difference between managing a place where 17 people leave in one month vs. one person. The second option is a cakewalk. The first feels like a four-alarm fire. You barely have time to douse the flames sprouting around you, much less find, hire, and train all those replacements. When you do manage to hire someone, they'll be surrounded by frenetic People who don't have time to smile, much less help the new guy. Chaos is a terrible environment in which to train or onboard an employee.

Momentum moves in both directions. Heavy turnover can result in a devastating downward spiral, as you lose traction and descend the mountain you're trying to climb. Training and retaining team members whose experience and buy-in multiply each week provides incredible drive as you climb toward your Pinnacle.

Playbooks are key for retention and the employee experience at Discover Strength, according to David Gschneidner. The training Playbook for new exercise physiologists at Discover includes an initial two-week checklist that's very specific day by day. Once new hires pass the two-week mark and are working on the floor, they use a more general weekly checklist for the next six months. After that training period, the practitioner seamlessly moves into plays that are part of the 10-year growth plan, which provides a clear path for development. These checklists include milestones for continuing education, certifications, and national accreditation.

"Having a core growth plan is a huge differentiator for us, especially in the fitness space," David says. "A lot of people in fitness are independent contractors and have a hard time with career planning and seeing a path forward. Even if they want to grow and educate themselves, they may not necessarily know the best route to take, so one of the things that attracts people to us is that they have a growth plan."

This is a terrific example of how Playbooks can build autonomy. Team members at Discover Strength control their own development — and their own raises, which are tied to the education, certification, longevity, and other benchmarks spelled out in the Playbook.

"You're not at the whim of your manager when it comes to your compensation," David says. "You can create your own future and decide, hey, I want to make X amount of money. You know how to get there. People understand the path, and so, the growth plan is huge for our retention."

One of Discover Strength's core values, by the way, is "Creating our own future," so the growth plan is one of the ways Playbooks can build culture as a business uses them to fulfill Purpose and climb toward their Pinnacle.

BUILD VALUE

While playbooks build value for customers and employees, they also build the value of the company in concrete terms. The more dependent the business is on you as the entrepreneur, the less valuable it is. Buyers want to know they can close on a business and run it smoothly from the start. Many small to medium-sized businesses, though, follow a model that business guru Jim Collins calls "one genius with 1,000 helpers." It's all about the owner or CEO, in which case, a buyer must clamp golden handcuffs on the visionary leader and keep them around to realize any value.

> *" **THE MORE DEPENDENT THE BUSINESS IS ON YOU AS THE ENTREPRENEUR, THE LESS VALUABLE IT IS.** *

The genius label might boost an ego, but as a system — or non-system — it's no fun. Do you want to be indispensable, or have a business that runs smoothly even if you get sick, take a long vacation, or sell? A well-run business is a self-managing business, and Playbooks can help you get there.

Playbooks are *the* key factor in getting your business to run like that proverbial well-oiled machine, which is the heart of every entrepreneur's dream. As their analogues do in sports, our Playbooks set the stage for Performance. Once great coaches have solid plays, they work on conditioning and practice to coax great Performances from the team. In Chapter 5, we'll explore powerful ways to boost Performance, from mentoring tools to a weekly scoreboard (did we "Win the Week?") to superior meeting structures.

Playbooks lay the groundwork, Performance is where the magic happens.

MOUNTAIN LOOKBACK

- **Better Performance / Workflows.** Processes run better when those performing them have a Playbook of uniform "plays," or essential checklists, to guide them through steps.

- **Better Processes.** A Playbooks initiative means analyzing and optimizing key processes across the organization, so the whole business runs better.

- **Customer Experience.** Playbooks hold all team members to a uniform standard, so clients get consistent service. They "systemize the predictable so you can humanize the exceptional."

- **Onboarding / Training.** Having all relevant plays for every process they touch, allows team members to train better and faster, setting them up for success.

- **Employee Experience.** Playbooks set clear expectations and standards, which is the kind of clarity and accountability A-players want. They establish alignment, cut friction, and boost teamwork as we climb, united.

- **Retention.** The smoother daily processes run, thanks to Playbooks, the longer team members will stay. The clear expectations and development path spelled out in Playbooks are two of the many ways they help you retain A-players.

- **Coaching.** Good coaching is impossible without clear documentation of process. The tribal-knowledge approach means half a dozen versions for each process. Playbooks set one standard and help team members to align, so the business runs like a machine.

- **Company value.** No one pays a premium for a business that needs its current owner or CEO to run. Playbooks allow the company to manage itself — and allow the visionary leader to go on vacation, recover from illness, or sell without worry.

CHAPTER 5

PERFORMANCE

COACH YOUR TEAM TO A STAR PERFORMANCE

If ever there was a legacy business that could afford to rest on its laurels, you'd have thought it was Park Chrysler Jeep, in Burnsville, MN. The successful dealership has been owned by the same family since it opened in 1957. It is firmly embedded in the community, where some neighbors have bought cars from the company for generations during its nearly 70 years in business.

But brothers Jonathan and David Dworsky, the second generation of Dworskys to run Park Chrysler Jeep, aren't the type of leaders for whom good enough is good enough. After assuming leadership roles, they joined Vistage, the CEO coaching and peer advisory group. They read business books and looked for ways to improve systems and boost Performance at the organization.

"My brother and I believe you have to grow and elevate your leadership and discipline over time," Jonathan Dworsky says. "It became clear to us that we needed to take another look at our core competencies, our leadership team, the organization of the company, accountability, people — all the things you have to define to improve performance and create a culture that's engaging."

That quest for excellence ramped up after the Great Recession of 2008.

"We were just at a place where we had to start looking at things differently, so it wasn't hard to get buy-in," Jonathan says. "You get buy-in when you have to. It was a challenging time to be an auto dealer, especially through Chrysler. We felt we almost had to reinvent ourselves to be relevant."

I feel privileged to have played the role of Guide during that reinvention for nearly a decade now. Together, we worked on People, from frontline workers to leaders, with a focus on finding and keeping A-players. Jonathan and David realized that to boost team members' Performance, they had to boost their own, with powerful Playbooks for onboarding, training, assessment, and communication.

Pinnacle tools have helped us address those areas, as well as culture. Park Chrysler Jeep leaders decided that their Purpose is "Building timeless relationships" (it was always there, we just had to articulate it). They established core values and a Pinnacle goal of being "Powered by Exceptional Moments." They wrote a detailed code of conduct, which all team members sign and then see every day at the dealership, where it's posted (everything from a professional presence to teamwork is covered).

CODE OF CONDUCT

1. Professional Presence

a. Arrive punctually and prepared for your shift.

b. Maintain a professional appearance when clocking in.

c. Cell phones should be used strictly for business purposes while at work.

d. Speakerphones may be used behind closed doors.

e. Earbuds are not allowed in customer areas.

f. Smoking, chewing, or vaping is permitted only in designated smoking areas.

g. If you use tobacco products, please wash your hands, and freshen your breath.

2. Awareness of Hospitality Environment

a. Stay attentive to your surroundings.

b. Engage in professional conversations.

c. Always acknowledge guests before they acknowledge you.

d. Offer customers a beverage and a snack.

e. Hold the door open for others, including vehicles.

f. Avoid gathering in customer-facing areas to maintain a professional atmosphere.

3. Warm Welcome to All

a. Make eye contact, smile, and welcome everyone.

b. Accompany and introduce customers to the person they are looking for.

c. Address customers by their title and surname (e.g., Mrs. Jones), unless directed otherwise by the guest.

4. Professional & Courteous Communication

a. Refrain from using profanity.

b. Discuss customer information privately when it is business-related.

c. Use an appropriate volume and tone when speaking.

5. Always Do The Right Thing

a. Take ownership of any complaints received.

6. Be a Team Player

a. Maintain open communication with team members.

b. Refer to sales department members as "Product Specialists" during introductions.

c. Support your coworkers.

7. Knowledge Sharing and Pride

a. Have a thorough understanding of our products, including vehicles, service, parts, detail, and internal processes.

b. Continuously seek learning opportunities.

8. Expressing Appreciation

a. Always respond with "My Pleasure."

b. Acknowledge and welcome returning guests.

c. Extend the invitation for guests to visit us again.

9. Value our Reputation

a. Ambassadors of Park Chrysler Jeep

b. Your actions are a reflection of our image.

10. Contributing to Facility Splendor

a. Wash your hands before entering common areas or customers' vehicles after working in the shop or detail area.

b. Enhance our appearance by promptly picking up debris.

c. Handle tools and equipment with care.

d. Report any necessary repairs promptly.

e. Prioritize the safety of all individuals at all times.

We kindly ask every member of our team to wholeheartedly commit to upholding the principles outlined in our Code of Conduct. By adhering to these guidelines, we can collectively create a professional, welcoming, and exceptional environment for our guests and colleagues alike. Let us embrace these standards as ambassadors of our organization, demonstrating integrity, respect, and a dedication to providing the utmost in service and care. Together, we can contribute to the ongoing success and splendor of Park Chrysler Jeep.

David & Jonathan Dworsky

Park Chrysler Jeep
Since 1957

We also worked on more effective meetings, understanding that they are "the fuel that runs the engine," as Jonathan says, an apt metaphor for his business. Those improved meetings became one of the Dworskys' key methods for tracking not just individual Performance but overall company Performance, too, through our Strategic Vision & Execution Plan, a key Pinnacle tool that maps out goals, milestones, and "Rocks" — the quarterly goals that get us to those larger ones.

How did all those efforts to boost Performance pay off at the dealership that others might have treated as a sleepy lifestyle business?

Park Chrysler Jeep consistently ranks number one or two in Jeep sales in its highly competitive market. That's especially impressive, considering that the independently owned business is mostly battling multi-dealer groups. Park Chrysler Jeep has grown exponentially, up to 122 employees as I write this, and the dealership built its "dream facility," which doubled the size of the old one (34 bays now, up from 16).

The obvious metrics that impress outside observers, though, matter less to Jonathan than the internal ones that produce those tangible results.

"Sales, growth, net profit — all those things are important, and we do well in them, but we're on the high end of the performance scale in what we do operationally," Jonathan says. "That's really important — and the biggest testament to our success is our clients' response. We rank really high in repeat business and referrals."

After improving Performance in myriad ways, Park Chrysler Jeep once again might seem in a position to coast. David and Jonathan don't see it that way. They have a new set of goals involving market share, service volume, and People — an effort to boost Performance further by "leveling up" current players and hiring more A-players.

"We find that when a business grows exponentially like ours did, you can just put the same structure inside a new building, but the building doesn't change things," Jonathan says. "You'll have the same problems. Fortunately, we had a great foundation with Pinnacle, which gave us the tools to have an evolving structure — business analysis and people analysis. As you expand, you have to keep reevaluating processes, job duties, organization, everything."

PERFORMANCE STARTS WITH LEADERS

In this chapter, we'll explore Performance — actual work, concrete action, the things teams do to create tangible results. Our first three principles — People, Purpose, and Playbooks — set the stage for star Performance, but leaders must coach their teams to it. Great Performance doesn't just happen. Our first three fundamental principles create the conditions that make it possible, but only smart leadership, coaching, and communication get you over the line.

I started with the story of David and Jonathan Dworsky because they understand that good enough isn't good enough. Getting to excellence in Performance requires serious effort, and as Jonathan demonstrates, maintaining it demands vigilance. If you're not moving forward, you're falling behind. There's no resting on laurels with Performance, and in today's economy, there's no such thing as a lifestyle business that can simply coast while Performing poorly, at least not for very long. As sales guru Zig Ziglar says, the only way to coast is downhill.

Ziglar's pronouncement is truer now than ever. Every day that your business operates, sales atrophy and expenses rise. These are the facts of life in the 21st century, as certain as aging and taxes. To put it in the simplest terms, your job as a leader is to fight that natural inertia, to push up sales and push down expenses in order to create a margin, some of which feeds Profit and some of which helps you maintain a strong culture and pay A-players what they're worth. Our goals as Guides is to help you stay focused on the vital few rather than the trivial many. It's easy to get caught up in the daily whirlwind and chaos, and forget that business comes down to just a few simple disciplines practiced over and over again.

Strong Performance is a necessity for making a Profit, even for surviving, long-term. You might limp along in a particular niche in the near term with subpar Performance, but it leaves you vulnerable. One disruption — one big new competitor, technology, or economic headwind — and you can slump into unprofitability, even obsolescence.

Can't happen to you?

That's what cabdrivers in Manhattan thought well into the 2000s. In early 2014, New York City taxi medallions (the license to operate a cab) sold for more than $1 million, reflecting the limited number of these cash cows, which enjoyed bottomless demand no matter how poor the service. By 2015, after Uber and Lyft took hold — with their clean cars and dazzling apps — those medallions had lost almost half their value. By 2021, they sold for under $80,000.

The Chicago Tribune was such a media behemoth, its salespeople didn't have to sell advertising — they simply took orders. As the threat of online competition grew, The Tribune Company decided — many days late and many dollars short — to dump millions into poorly conceived and managed tech initiatives that resulted in a whole lot of nothing. *The Tribune's* 2008 bankruptcy was the largest filing in the history of American media.

Small retailers who have upped their Performance by offering a higher level of service, unique immersive experiences, a sense of community, and other perks have survived Amazon while thousands of fellow storeowners shut down amid slumping sales, many after decades in business.

Forgive the gloomy examples, but I want to highlight the idea that Performance is not the cherry on top or the extra star in an online review. It is the thing that makes you money — no accident that this chapter flows into Chapter 6, on Profit. Performance is the thing that allows you to thrive once you've started addressing People, Purpose, and Playbooks. Most readers, I know, understand this. In my experience, good leaders trying to build and run healthy businesses realize the importance of Performance. They want to improve it and usually have made valiant attempts, but like climbers after a heavy rain, they get stuck on the mountainside, taking two sloppy steps forward and three back, the elusive Pinnacle distant as ever.

Leaders are not sure where to start, what measures to take, what resources they need to boost Performance as comprehensively as the Dworskys have at Park Chrysler.

I'll discuss an effective systematic approach to boosting Performance that builds on our previous three principles, but first, find a good mirror, because the effort starts with you. There's an inclination with Performance to lament outside forces — poor employee engagement, a shrinking labor pool, lack of initiative, a shoddy work ethic, or more broadly, an entire generation (*those millennials, that Gen Z, the kids today*...take your pick). Excuse my French, but that's all b.s.

Great Performance starts with great leaders, and to borrow an idea from W. Edwards Deming, your business and team are Performing at the precise level you have designed them to Perform at. Don't start with their Performance but your own. When a sports team has a string of terrible seasons, who gets fired?

The coach, of course. A business runs on the same principle, and for better or worse, the buck stops with you.

The Pinnacle Talent Assessment, which I introduced in Chapter 2, on People, asks for simple ratings of team members on culture and productivity, but I always start the exercise by asking leaders to rate themselves. After a few minutes, we go around the room to learn that the top executives at the company are giving themselves scores of 8 and 7, sometimes lower. *I'm an 8 on culture, but I really need to spend more time in the field and figure out supply chain issues, so I'm a 7 on productivity these days,* says the Chief Experience Officer. *I'm an 8 on productivity, but I still haven't worked our core values into hiring or training Playbooks, so I'm a 7, maybe even a 6 on culture,* admits the COO, and so on...

Okay, there is your lid, I tell them. No one in the business can rate above the leaders at the top, the People running the organization. You have put that cap on Performance. John Maxwell calls this dynamic "the law of the lid," and as he points out, only leaders can lift it.

I start with this caveat because, obviously, there's no point in trying to boost team members' Performance, urging them up the mountain if you, as a leader, camp at the halfway mark. Everyone wants to ascend the peaks with a great leader, and that's what you have to aspire to as your own Performance evolves. If you rate 7 in culture and 7 in productivity this year, aim for 8s next year. You must continually improve because like the business, you can't coast without heading downhill, and your Performance sets the tone for the whole organization.

The inverse of the law of the lid — we might call it the law of the climb — says that leaders whose own Performance remains on an upward trajectory can lift the team to ever higher peaks. If you rate a 7 this year in culture, as I said, you want to be at least an 8 next year, but as culture improves throughout the organization, the standard rises. A rating of 7 in 2025 at Park Chrysler Jeep, with its current initiatives and A-players in a facility that has doubled in size, means more than a 7 did in 2023. At a thriving business, the scale itself continually evolves.

If Performance is not a priority for leaders, it won't be for others, and the effort is doomed. Leaders have to feel that gap that drives motivation in all our lives — the distance from *Cs* to *As* in school, from 230 pounds to 180, from single life to family life, from busboy to assistant manager. You know what I mean, or you would not be reading this book. You have followed me all the way to Chapter 5 because you want your business to Perform better.

What's causing that gap in Performance? Where is the organization currently and where should it be? How do you get there?

I'll provide tools and methods here that help you answer these questions, building on the three fundamentals we've covered in depth. The stage is set: we have the right People on the bus in the right seats with a clear Purpose and a Pinnacle to climb toward. We have solid Playbooks to optimize our processes. Now, it's showtime, gameday, the hour for action, coaching, rewards, and recognition.

The first step is to see where you are.

ASSESS YOUR CURRENT ELEVATION

Discover Strength uses an egg-like capsule called The Bod Pod to measure the percentage of a person's body weight that's composed of muscle vs. fat and to record their resting metabolic rate — information that's useful in prescribing the right workout and caloric intake.

At Pinnacle Business Guides, we have our own version of the Bod Pod for companies called The Baseline Assessment©. It's one of the tools I'm most proud of because it's easy to use, takes all of 10 minutes, and is incredibly helpful. Leaders answer 20 questions, rating their company from weak to strong on each. We analyze their answers and then provide a PDF report with an overall score for organizational health, as well as individual scores on each of our five fundamental principles.

Leaders can see at a glance, for instance, if they're Performing well in terms of People and Playbooks but need to work on Purpose or Profits. A color-coded pie-chart turns your scores in each area into a rich visual that reveals where you're excelling and lagging. Something about seeing your Performance broken down by principle on the page is particularly edifying. *We're at 90 percent on People — a very strong score — but only 50 percent on Playbooks? We're shooting our team in its collective foot!*

Each section of the report — organized according to the five principles — then highlights recommendations and tools that can help you act on them. If, for instance, you need to Perform better in People by hiring more A-players and clarifying expectations, we might suggest our Talent Assessment, A-Players Draft, and Hire the Right Who© tools. If under Purpose, your Brand Story and Inspiration show weakness, we could recommend Discovering Your Flywheel© tool and other tools to help you appreciate and communicate the things you do best.

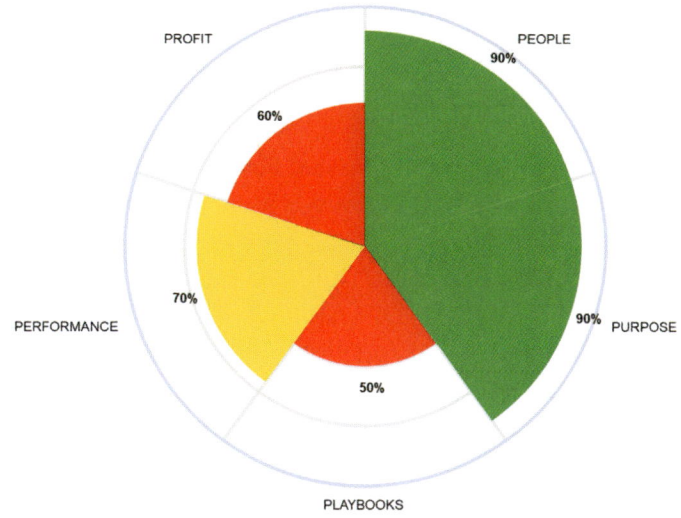

Of course, you can talk to a Pinnacle Business Guide about your Baseline Assessment results and begin a deeper analysis, but you can also act on the recommendations on your own and begin improving Performance immediately. The Baseline Assessment and report are free and can be accessed at: PinnacleBusinessGuides.com. I love this tool because apart from providing leaders with specific recommendations that improve Performance, it gets them thinking about their business in terms of the five fundamental principles that cover all aspects of organizational health.

Anyone who wants to lose weight starts the journey on a scale, right? If I want to get down to 180 pounds, I have to know I'm starting at 210 and need to lose 30 — otherwise, I can't track progress. Want better grades or to run a faster mile? You start, of course, by noting your current GPA or timing your current mile. Measuring Performance requires benchmarks that reveal where you're starting and how far you have to climb. The Baseline Assessment offers a good overall benchmark to begin the ascent, and another Pinnacle tool I'll briefly explain, The Brutal Facts, drills down into daily Performance gaps in more detail, as it also helps leaders to determine their current elevation.

This tool, which Pinnacle Business Guides introduce to leaders on day one of Base Camp, is adapted from what Jim Collins, in his business classic *Good to Great: Why Some Companies Make the Leap...And Others Don't,* calls "the Stockdale Paradox," after Admiral James Stockdale. During his seven years as a POW at the Hanoi Hilton, Stockdale both acknowledged his brutal reality and believed wholeheartedly that he would eventually transcend it. This sort of duality, Collins argues, is a hallmark of companies whose Performance goes from good to great:

"You must maintain unwavering faith that you can and will prevail in the end, regardless of the difficulties," Collins writes, "AND *at the same time* have the discipline to confront the most brutal facts of your current reality, whatever they might be."[1]

Keeping the Stockdale Paradox in mind, we use this tool to solicit from leaders the Brutal Facts confronting their organization. Our Guides consider this tool one of the greatest immediate services we can provide for leadership teams. When psychologists study how People want bad news or unpleasant information delivered, most say they want it straight, direct, no beating around the bush. And yet, when leaders deliver bad news or discuss uncomfortable topics, transparency surrenders to delay and indirection — *never on a Friday, never before lunch, soften the message by couching it in language that...*

Our Brutal Facts tool cuts through the reluctance and obfuscation, creating a safe space for leaders to address problems head-on. We start by asking, what are the Brutal Facts we

---

1   Jim Collins, *Good to Great: Why Some Companies Make the Leap...And Others Don't,* (HarperCollins Publishers Inc., 2001) 13.

need to address as a company? What is not working? What's holding us back? What is frustrating you and stopping us from growing? We remind everyone that we're only interested in facts here, not opinions. *We don't pay people enough* is an opinion. *Our compensation is 20 percent below our competitors* is a fact. *The warehouse is understaffed* is an opinion. *The warehouse is handling 10 percent more product with 20 percent fewer workers, and overtime has doubled* is a fact.

Every leader must write down five Brutal Facts, jotting each on a large sticky note. Team members stick all their Brutal Facts on the wall — often 50 or 60 — then sorts them into clusters, grouping those that seem related or belong under the same umbrella. Each of those clusters gets labeled with a name that describes the general category. Together, the team then prioritizes the clusters, and finally, establishes goals and FAST Rocks (more on these shortly) to address them.

The clarity that emerges from the airing of Brutal Facts is nothing short of magical. The discussions that accompany our sorting into clusters, the prioritizing and goal-setting, can be more productive than a year of strategic meetings.

While using this tool, we keep our eye on the Pinnacle — Stockdale's faith that we will prevail — but we also determine our current elevation, the boulders in our way, the grade of the mountain, and the best route forward. There's always some sighing and headshaking during this exercise, as we reveal all the places where our Performance lags, but by the time we've completed The Brutal Facts, leaders are energized and excited to climb. Some of these issues have lingered unaddressed for months, even years. Some have never been categorized, or even named. It's a relief for leaders to finally express their frustrations, label problems, and leave with a concrete plan for addressing them.

Here's another magical thing about The Brutal Facts: those clusters of related items that we create and then label? They pretty much always fall into five fundamental categories. I'll let you guess what they are, but hint: they all start with "P."

COACH, DON'T MANAGE

It all starts with People, I wrote early in this book, and "all" certainly includes Performance. Our fourth fundamental principle, the one that leads directly into Profit, obviously depends on People. They are the ones who get it done, play the game, and complete the work, the ones who move us inch by inch up the mountain — no matter how harsh the weather or how steep the climb.

Of course, leaders want People in their organization to Perform to the absolute best of their ability, and no one wants a star Performance more than team members themselves. And yet, as with the organization as a whole, we experience serious gaps in individual Performance. In fact, those gaps often add up to the larger ones showing up in our company's Baseline Assessment — and bottom line. Cumulatively, they're behind most of the Brutal Facts we face day to day.

Boosting the Performance of individual contributors is a complex, never-ending job. I began this chapter by enumerating the many ways David and Jonathan Dworsky boosted Performance at Park Chrysler Jeep, yet in 2025, as I write this, one of their chief goals is to hire more A-players and "level up" the current players who linger in B and C territory. These are leaders who are doing exceptionally well on all five principles, but improving individual Performance still takes a concerted daily effort.

That effort can be downright depressing for leaders who are also dealing with financial shortfalls, competitive threats, shifting economic winds, and all manner of headaches. Too often, leaders accept mediocre Performance because they can't afford the time or energy to deal with the individuals churning it out. It's a circular argument, of course, because they would have much more time and energy if only they could boost team members' Performance.

They get stuck at this Performance gap — crevasse might be a better term — mid-climb because they simply don't have the tools to cross it. The things they've tried aren't working, and so, they accept the status quo. Good enough becomes good enough.

One of the keys to crossing that crevasse and boosting individual Performance is to stop thinking like a manager and start thinking like a coach. Like great coaches, leaders need to give team members excellent Playbooks and a sense of Purpose, as we've discussed. They need to regularly assess today's Performance and clearly articulate how it can improve tomorrow. They must oversee the kinds of rigorous practice that will get team members to the next level, help them track the numbers that mark their progress, and have frank conversations that set expectations.

As I said, this effort is complex and, I think, almost impossible without effective tools. I am biased, of course — I believe Pinnacle Business Guide's People and Performance tools are the best available. We've developed a deep, sophisticated toolbox, and we're flexible about adapting our tools to a company's particular needs and using outside tools when necessary. Most operating systems, though, have quality tools for boosting Performance, and sometimes companies have good homegrown tools, too, though these often leave gaps. Whether you use ours, your own, or someone else's, you need effective tools if you're serious about improving Performance, just as serious climbers know they need a rope, crampons, and ladder to cross a crevasse.

I already described a couple of the most important tools we use for boosting individuals' Performance in Chapter 2, on People, so I'll just give a quick reminder here. The first, our Talent Assessment — one of our bedrock tools — does for individuals what the Baseline Assessment does for the whole business.

Those we place in the graph's top right quadrant are A-players, scoring high for both culture and productivity. We need to pay them what they're worth and make sure they have the resources and encouragement to continue turning in a star Performance. You'll recall from Chapter 2 that A-players are free. These People are skilled, productive, and not just onboard with your culture, but willing to go the extra mile to serve your Purpose and get up the mountain. They are the believers, and, ultimately, free because no matter what you pay them, they contribute more than they take.

In Chapter 2, I mentioned Steve Jobs' famous assertion that much of his success depended on hiring A-players, who propagate themselves once they reach critical mass. A-players want to work with A-players. The Dworskys, as I said, have made recruiting A-players such a priority at Park Chrysler Jeep that together, we created a list of "What A-Players Want," which I'll share below. Anyone who hires People at your organization should get this list tattooed somewhere prominent! Okay, posting it over their desk is probably sufficient, but take it from Steve Jobs — it's hard to overestimate the power of aiming for A-players.

What "A Players" Want from the Leaders of Park Jeep

1. Challenge and Growth: A Players thrive on being challenged. They want leaders who push them to exceed their limits and achieve more, whether it's solving complex problems or handling high-stakes situations. In every department—from Sales and Service to Parts and Finance—these individuals expect clear accountability, and leaders who take decisive action to help them grow.

2. Clear Expectations and Accountability: High performers appreciate clarity. They expect their leaders to set clear expectations and mutual agreements that outline specific goals and hold them accountable for achieving those goals. Accountability is essential for them to feel they are progressing, and they respect leaders who are consistent in taking action and addressing both successes and areas for improvement.

3. Positive Reinforcement and Recognition: While A Players are self-motivated, they still value recognition. They want leaders who provide positive reinforcement when they excel, acknowledging their hard work and contributions across the dealership. This recognition, whether public or private, fuels their desire to keep improving.

4. Collaboration with Other "A Players": A Players perform best when surrounded by other high achievers. They want to work in an environment where they can collaborate with and learn from their peers, creating a culture where top performers elevate each other.

5. Trust and Autonomy: A Players want trust in their abilities. They seek autonomy in their roles, whether managing customer relationships, diagnosing complex vehicle issues, or navigating intricate finance deals. Leaders who trust them and provide opportunities for them to shine without micromanagement will see them excel.

6. Growth and Development Path: A clear growth and development map that includes regular training and coaching is critical for A Players. They want to know there is a plan for their continued professional development, and they expect leaders to invest in their future. Offering learning opportunities and coaching tailored to their needs makes them feel valued and supported.

7. Environment and Tools to Succeed: A Players expect an environment equipped with the right tools and resources to achieve success. Whether it's advanced diagnostic technology for technicians, streamlined software for finance, or customer engagement tools for sales, the right environment is essential for them to perform at their best.

8. Open Communication, Clear Vision, and Direction: Transparency is key for A Players. They want leaders who communicate openly and honestly about the dealership's direction and long-term goals. A clear vision and direction help them understand how their roles contribute to the bigger picture. Regular feedback, honest conversations, and open communication around both successes and challenges are essential to keeping A Players engaged and aligned with the dealership's mission.

In summary "A Players" want to work with "A Players." Hire "A Players!"

"B Player" leaders hire "C Players."

By incorporating these elements, leaders at Park Jeep can build a culture where A Players are continuously engaged, supported, and motivated to drive the dealership's success across all departments.

Consider this: Do you have the team you deserve?

Those team members in the other three quadrants of our Talent Assessment should either be coached to a higher level — the Cs up to Bs and the Bs to As — or invited to leave the bus. To make this determination, we use the "Level Up" tool also described in Chapter 2. If you recall, this exercise helps leaders to a gut-check on who Performs like a rock star and who Performs so poorly, they're probably not worth trying to save.

How do you coach a B or C-player to become a star Performer? The language we use — "coach," not manage or supervise — offers a clue. Like great coaches, leaders should start by making sure People know their own numbers. Good athletes always know their numbers — their RBI, rushing stats, time in the 100-meter, assists, rebounds, etc. They track the slightest movements and trends in those numbers and obsess over how to improve them.

One of the most important baseline numbers for every employee is their score on the Talent Assessment. If Kelly is a 9 on productivity but barely a 5 on culture, that disparity should be addressed and explored in our quarterly coaching sessions (more on these shortly). A good coach will help Kelly come up with a plan to raise that culture score and reach an agreement with her on specific targets — *so, we agree that your culture score should be at least a 6 by our next quarterly coaching conversation, in three months, and we're aiming for a 7 by next year.*

Note that we're forming an "agreement," not an "expectation." We often talk about "expectations" in trying to improve Performance, but that term implies a one-way, top-down standard dropped on someone. An agreement is a mutual understanding arrived at by two parties. It involves give and take, and because of that, achieves buy-in. The terms of that agreement call for Kelly to go from a 5 to a 7 on culture over the course of a year — ambitious but gradual. No one buys running shoes and enters a marathon the same day. We all need time to improve our Performance, whether we're working on music, weight loss, marketing, or sales. Unrealistic *expectations* can do more harm than good — so stick with gradual, realistic *agreements*.

AGREEMENTS NOT EXPECTATIONS

When it comes to improving Performance, we often rely on "expectations," but that term implies a one-way, top-down standard that we impose on someone. An agreement is a mutual understanding arrived at by two parties. It involves give and take, and because of that, achieves buy-in. The terms of the agreement in our example call for Kelly to go from a 5 to a 7 on culture over the course of a year — ambitious but gradual progress. No one buys running shoes and enters a marathon the same day. We all need time to improve our Performance, whether we're working on music, weight loss, marketing, or sales. Unrealistic *expectations* can do more harm than good — so stick with gradual, realistic *agreements*.

WIN THE WEEK

What other numbers, besides our Talent Assessment, are key for team members? What are the handful of metrics they should obsess over, wake up thinking about, and strategize all week to improve? Nobody wants the vague praise of "good job" or "atta boy" — least of all the A-players you must keep happy. They want to know exactly how or why their Performance was terrific or fell short. They want hard targets, not vague imperatives like "sell more" or "increase margins." What does that even mean?

The numbers that matter, of course, will depend on your business. If you're a law office, maybe you aim for 85 percent billable hours, three new intake calls, or four demand letters out the door. If you're in construction, maybe you'd like three bids sent, three new opportunities in the pipeline, or one deal closed. The leaders at Discover Strength, the personal training business we've discussed, are serious former athletes, so they take naturally to using key numbers to boost Performance. Two of their key metrics are sessions per trainer and sessions per location. These are numbers everyone at the company keeps an eye on.

Note that my examples are simple, specific, and activity-based. Focusing on activities gives team members control and focuses attention on the efforts that will result in long-term outcomes, without shaming anybody for those inevitable tough weeks. If I hit my 15 appointments, 100 cold calls, 25 marketing packets mailed with customized letters...my Performance will get there, just as hitting the gym four days a week or running five miles every other day inevitably shows results.

We're essentially talking about KPIs here, Key Performance Indicators, though in my lexicon, the acronym stands for Kept Promise Indicators. *When you hired me, I promised certain things — I would grow the client base, get new business, retain clients*, etc. What numbers reflect how well I'm keeping those promises week by week? How many new clients have I brought in? What's my percentage on retention? If the numbers are too complex or vague, you've already lost. We are trying to *gamify* weekly Performance, to continue our coaching metaphor, to stoke the spirit of competition, the quest for glory — and to make it fun.

Because the only way to get up the mountain is as a team, we also need to track numbers for every department, office, store, location — whatever units make sense for your business. Our "Win the Week" tool is essentially a scoreboard that leaders customize, identifying key Performance numbers for each team. What does it look like for your department to Win the Week? Think about the numbers that matter most and post how we're doing.

Again, keep your Win the Week scoreboard activity-based, simple, and specific. You must be able to answer, based on solid data, *yes* or *no* to the question, did we Win the Week? If we did, we check that box on the scoreboard and celebrate. If we didn't, we check *no* and come back hungry next week. At Discover Strength, for instance, each location Wins the Week if it did more sessions than it completed the previous week. So simple, so elegant! If we're a new location and did 36 sessions last week, it takes 37 to Win the Week, while at more mature locations, the Performance standard might be in the hundreds. The number of houses shown, calls processed, customers served, prospects phoned, lines of code written — whatever your key weekly metric is, get it on the scoreboard and coach your team to a win.

Each team member's numbers and their contribution to the scoreboard then become talking points in our quarterly coaching conversations. Everyone should be meeting with a leader every 90 days for a coaching session (some new employees might even require weekly meetings for a while). As in a "review," we go over the previous 90 days' Performance in these one-on-one meetings, but unlike many reviews, the focus is not on judgement, reprimand, or praise. Instead, we want to collaborate on how each team member can Perform to the highest standard and contribute to our climb. As leaders, we share our ideas for boosting Performance but spend much of the session asking questions and soliciting feedback from the team member.

Our Quarterly Coaching Conversation tool incorporates our Talent Assessment for a discussion of culture and productivity, as I mentioned, and includes a series of questions on what's working and what isn't. The idea is to mentor, inspire, and engage through dialogue (reviews tend toward monologue). This might seem like common sense, but even many enlightened leaders who think they are engaging in constructive two-way conversations each quarter don't realize how negative the experience is or how much airtime they take up. Of course, there's room to improvise, but starting the session with standard questions — *What's working well? Where can you add more value to our team? What's frustrating our clients? What needs to be fixed?* — guarantees a two-way talk that engages team members, stoking a sense of ownership and Purpose. We don't ask such questions for form's sake, by the way, or solely to inspire. Every team member is another set of eyes with a unique view of the organization. They are a rich source of intelligence and often have great ideas for improving process — only no one's bothered to ask them.

Before we move on from quarterly coaching, I want to be clear that if someone is consistently underperforming, radical candor should be part of the conversation. Leaders have to point out exactly how and where People are falling short before they come to an agreement on a plan to coach them up. No one should ever be surprised when they get fired. Patrick Lencioni, as I've mentioned, calls a firing without ample warning "the last act of cowardice." If leaders let things get to the point that someone needs to exit the team and haven't had the hard conversations, that's on them, not the team member.

THE HERD
YOU DESERVE

Ask any pro sports coach — for that matter, any parent coaching a Pee Wee team — if overseeing practice is an important part of the job, and they'll think you're kidding. Practice essentially *is* the job when you're a coach, just as it is most of the job for pro sports players. NFL teams have just 17 regular season games, but they practice five to six days a week during the season and at training camp, with more training and practice off-season.

Actors rehearse for weeks and weeks before the curtain rises on a play, and for movie roles, shoot a single scene dozens of times before they get the actual take.

And in sales, marketing, customer service, installation? At many companies, you might get some quick practice during a training period for your job, and often, no more, ever. Unlike star athletes, experienced pros who have been performing their jobs in business for years and could devise their own practice regimens don't practice either. They are too good for practice, they think, which is curiously different from the mindset of Michael Jordan, Caitlin Clark, and Tom Brady. They have been pretty good at their jobs, too, and continued to practice mani-acally. One might even surmise that their attitudes toward practice — so different from the ones we find in the business world — were a factor in their success.

Quality Performance demands practice, even of prodigies, so companies that want to make it up the mountain had better rehearse the climb. People are reluctant to arrange regular practice for their teams or to practice themselves partly because they haven't done much of it and partly because they're not sure what it should look like. Often, the idea simply hasn't occurred to them.

A client of mine, a $12 billion bank, recently gave a presentation in its effort to take over management of a pension fund, a major piece of business. The presentation went terribly. By leaders' own description, they missed the mark and didn't make much of an impression. They know their stuff and are well positioned for the win, but they did not practice. As I write this, they are scheduled to return and present again. In preparation, they are now laboring over every slide, carefully describing the problems they'll solve, and practicing the presentation from start to finish.

Anyone giving an important presentation should practice it before peers first, no doubt about it. Leadership should arrange such sessions, and if they don't, team members should arrange their own. But the prevalent attitude, astonishingly, is, I can't wait to go to the presentation to see what I'll say.

I have trained enough salespeople in my career to populate a small country, so no one knows better than I do that they hate to roleplay — and that it helps them enormously. At one company I worked with, I suspected that the 10 or so salespeople on payroll weren't giving great presentations. I suggested that over the next 10 weeks, we should have one salesperson per week come in and present to the leadership team. Two people quit rather than do a presentation, knowing how terribly it would go. The ones who did present improved markedly, even after the feedback generated from a single practice.

Practice sessions can be arranged for most work — customer service, budgeting, home appraisals, ad campaigns...Virtually everything can be practiced, whether that involves roleplaying, a dry run, or more creative methods. We have a wealth of technology today, including excellent video cameras on our phones, so we can watch ourselves and others performing tasks. Programs allow us to quickly test several versions of a slide deck on an audience, and calls can be recorded with one click and replayed for pointers.

After decades in business, I still practice all the time. A couple weeks ago, I recorded a call with a leader as he gave me thoughts about what his business needs and what others on the leadership team think about hiring Pinnacle Business Guides. I replayed that call and rehearsed my presentation before flying to meet the team last week. At this point, I could present on Pinnacle blindfolded with a head wound while chugging cough syrup, but that recording and practice made me better.

Tom Brady orchestrated some incredible plays with seconds to go because he practiced for those tough situations. Team members and businesses as a whole can do the same thing. Practice for those tough times, for economic downturns, for the loss of a major client, for do-or-die presentations, and the kind of customer service that resembles triage.

One of our Guides, David Quick, often says, "You have the herd you deserve." The idea is that when a storm approaches, cows and sheep hunker down and get skittish. Buffalo charge toward the storm to get through it faster. When there's a threat, they run at it, facing any challenge head-on.

Practice fosters a buffalo culture and the kind of clutch Performance that becomes a huge competitive advantage for a company, especially if your competitors respond like sheep when danger appears. *The economy's down, competition is fierce, interest rates are up? Okay, team, let's take to the hill! We can do this. We practiced for this.*

Cows run away from the storm while the buffalo charges toward it – and gets through it quicker.

As football legend Bear Bryant said, "It's not the will to win, but the will to prepare to win that makes the difference."

TRACKING PERFORMANCE

Practice is one of the ways we successfully achieve goals, which are the heart of Performance. Unlike role-playing and rehearsal, goals get no shade in business. Everyone understands their importance, though they often aren't structured or tracked optimally.

At Pinnacle, we call our quarterly goals "Rocks," a term developed by Stephen Covey, as many readers probably know. In case you aren't familiar with his metaphor, Covey argues that our days get filled up with minutiae — emails, unimportant phone calls, paperwork, administrative tasks, etc. — until there isn't enough time and energy left for the important stuff. He represents the important stuff as large rocks and the unimportant stuff as pebbles or gravel. In demonstrations, he dumps all his gravel in a bucket and, of course, the bigger rocks won't fit on top — they spill over. If, however, he puts the big rocks in first, the gravel then spills around them efficiently and everything fits. The message is, take care of the important stuff first — your Rocks — and you'll then find space for all the smaller tasks, too.

For decades, People in business talked about SMART Rocks, meaning goals that are Specific, Measurable, Achievable, Relevant, and Time-bound. In 2018, research out of MIT demonstrated that FAST goals work better. Here's the newer, more effective paradigm:

F — *Frequently reviewed* goals, researchers demonstrated, keep everyone focused. If you're not meeting weekly to see how a Rock is moving forward, it's likely to drift.

A — *Ambitious* Rocks are more successful than the low-level ones that are, say, tied to compensation; they should be doable but challenging. This minimizes the risk of sandbagging, or intentionally underperforming to lower the bar.

S — *Specific* — an obvious necessity for goals, since we need to know exactly what we're aiming for — this carries over from the SMART model. We must know what *done* looks like.

T — *Transparent* might be my favorite part of the revision of SMART to FAST. In the SMART Rocks paradigm, People in organizations unknowingly worked against each other — a salesman insisted we needed product here in two days instead of 14, while a controller worked to reduce inventory in the warehouse. When your goals are transparent — a strong meeting structure helps here — you work as a team, not at cross-purposes.

F.A.S.T. ROCK PLANNER

ROCK OWNER: **DUE DATE:**

ROCK TITLE:

DESCRIBE THE ROCK. WHAT DOES "DONE" LOOK LIKE?

Why is this ROCK important?

ROCK STEPS

BY DATE	ACTIVITY FOR COMPLETING THE ROCK	DATE COMPLETED
	First Step [+]	
	Mid-step [+]	
	Mid-step [+]	
	Mid-step [+]	
	Final Step [+]	

LIST RESOURCES NEEDED FOR COMPLETION

ROCK CLIMBING TIPS

1. Start early by identifying any obstacles that need to be overcome and resources needed to complete your Rocks.
2. Set benchmarks and review them in your weekly meetings to ensure that you stay on track.
3. Work as a team, communicate often, hold yourselves and each other accountable and help each other stay on track.
4. Think about the obstacles and how to overcome them. Sprint at the beginning of the quarter so you don't have to sprint at the end.
5. Are you being completely open and honest in your weekly meetings about the progress you're making on your Rocks?
   Are you willing to call out a peer if you sense that they're not really on track?

FREQUENTLY REVIEWED, **A**MBITIOUS, **S**PECIFIC, **T**RANSPARENT

PINNACLE

040422

I switched to FAST Rocks as soon as I read the MIT research and began teaching them to clients. Pinnacle takes the notion of FAST quite literally. At our Quarterly Summits, we help leadership teams decide on Rocks for the quarter — let's say there are six for Q2. We then assign a champion for each rock, somebody who will own it and shepherd it along. Leaders then take five or seven minutes to sketch out the Rocks they'll champion, using a wonderful tool we call the FAST Rock Planner. It helps them describe their Rock — why it's important, all its moving parts, and what *done* looks like. They write out milestones, list the resources needed for completion, etc. The magic happens when we have our FAST Rocks detailed and then go around the table, starting with number one, to discuss each, listening for alignment and clarity.

Several elements are worth pointing out here in terms of Performance. First, our method gets meat on the bones immediately, so leaders leave with fully developed Rocks, not a phrase or short sentence and an imperative to do the rest of the work...at some point. Second, the table talk for each Rock really puts the *Transparency* in FAST. If the top Rock is to develop an onboarding Playbook for new employees, Rachel, the Rock owner, will start by reading it aloud. The other leaders then ask questions and discuss her FAST Rock to make sure we're clear and aligned. *Rachel, are you going to do the background screening as part of this? Will your checklist include who the new person has lunch with that first week? How are we setting up their desks and who handles the welcome package? Why aren't business cards a part of this?* Everyone gets clarity on the goal and process. Rachel answers questions and explains her reasoning and, though she knows her Rocks, she inevitably revises and improves them with the aid of team input.

To keep our Rocks "frequently discussed," every leader then gives an update on their progress in our weekly tactical meetings.

Speaking of meetings...

They are, as Jonathan Dworsky says, the fuel that runs the engine of Performance. Actually, I'll go one further and say that they are business leaders' version of a stage. Every field has its stage — politicians have rallies, artists their gallery, street cops their beat, and teachers their classroom. In business, the meeting is our stage, and yet, leaders treat it as a chore or necessary evil. It is unconscionable that we've come to believe the activity most central to running our organizations is painful and unproductive. It does not have to be!

To improve your meetings, start by treating them as sacrosanct, not something to suffer through. Own the field, take control, and signal to all that this matters. Always have fresh markers and a clean whiteboard and test in advance any technology you plan to use (nothing kills momentum like 20 minutes spent trying to get an image onscreen). Everyone should know to dress appropriately, keep phones off, and listen attentively. If the junior varsity football team can follow meeting rules in the locker room, surely your leadership team can.

We want decorum — everyone should listen with an open mind and think before speaking — but also drama. This is a stage, remember, and a meeting without a certain amount of natural conflict is dull and unproductive. It fails as surely as a play or movie without conflict earns no audience investment. Ignoring differences and smoothing over arguments does not move us forward — it misses the whole point of a meeting. Instead, identify and nurture healthy conflict.

The other major problem with most meetings is that they lack context and Purpose. Meetings need clear agendas. To engage, team members need to know why meetings are taking place. The general staff meeting that covers everything under the sun, droning on for hours, is a disaster. The best way to create context is to clearly structure specific meetings for Purposes, establishing a particular time, cadence, and reason for each of our regular gatherings.

Pinnacle's Essential Meeting Structures© tool supplies three basic formats for vital meetings, which we encourage leaders to custom fit to their company and culture.

- **Standup**. Have a Standup meeting for 10-15 minutes daily (except on Fridays) to let colleagues know what you're working on and to learn what they're doing. This quick meeting keeps team members aligned and connected, and helps them execute faster, with a game plan for the day. Make this daily gathering "sticky" by giving it an odd time — 8:32 or 9:07 — and a quirky name — the Daily Huddle, the Scrum, Reveille, or whatever. The agenda is simply: what happened yesterday, what's happening today, and where do you need help?

- **Tactical**. This 90-minute weekly meeting replaces the Standup meeting one day a week to focus on priorities, debates, and execution. Here, we check on key numbers — did we Win the Week? — and update each other on FAST Rocks progress. It's a chance to be heard by and get help from the team, update each other on business development, review Rock accountability, revisit last week's issues, and prioritize this week's.

- **Financial & Rock Accountability**. Once a month, we substitute this financial agenda for one of our Tactical meetings to work on financial health and update each other on Rocks progress for two to four hours. We review the prior month's financials here, including the actual-vs.-budget variance report, the balance sheet, and 13-week cash flow. Leaders discuss progress and next steps on their Rocks, and we bring up one or two big topics that either improve our financial position or get Rocks back on track.

ESSENTIAL MEETING STRUCTURES Author: Gregory Cleary

Meetings are how leaders and managers execute the work, weigh in and buy in on how to get things done and keep everything on track and held together.

PINNACLE
BUSINESS GUIDES

SCAN TO DOWNLOAD

Strety, which I've mentioned, and Ninety are excellent software platforms for meetings and Pinnacle Preferred Partners. Both use a Pinnacle digital agenda that's connected to Rocks, our weekly scoreboard, fresh topics, carryover topics from last week's meeting, and other interactive metrics. This economical software is a great way to make the standard formats above work and tailor them to your needs. Both platforms have immense utility for keeping meetings on track, helping everyone to follow priorities, accountability, progress, and problems — and they show everyone that you're taking meetings seriously. Incorporating our meeting formats and the Pinnacle digital agenda through easily implemented software is like a tune-up for the whole organization that immediately boosts Performance and accountability.

Working on Performance, along with People, Purpose, and Playbooks, leads almost inevitably to our fifth principle, the culmination of all that effort — Profit. I say "almost" because Profit can't be taken for granted. We optimize it by figuring out what's worth pursuing and monitor it — and the company's vital signs — in creative ways. I'll introduce you to the tools and methods that help you enjoy and protect our fifth principle, the fruits of our labor, in the next chapter.

MOUNTAIN LOOKBACK

- **Performance Takes Work.** Our first 3 principles create conditions that make great Performance possible, but smart leadership, coaching, and communication get you over the line.

- **Leaders Are the Lid.** Your business and team are Performing at the precise level you have designed them to Perform at. Don't start with their Performance but your own.

- **Assess the Business.** Start improving Performance by determining your current elevation with a free Baseline Assessment at PinnacleBusinessGuides.com/Tools/Baseline-Assessment. Get benchmarked on organizational health and each of the 5 principles.

- **Assess Team Members.** Rate team members using our Talent Assessment. "Level Up" the B and C-players to higher Performance levels or ask them to leave.

- **Hire A-Players.** A-players are skilled, productive believers who help you scale. They're free because they give more than they take, so understand what they want and supply it.

- **Coach, Don't Manage.** Give team members their Talent Assessment scores and clear goals for improvement. Ask questions in quarterly coaching. Mentor, inspire, and engage through dialogue (reviews tend toward monologue).

- **Establish Agreements.** Establish *agreements*, which are mutual — not top-down *expectations*. Make radical candor a part of quarterly coaching when necessary. No one should be surprised to get fired.

- **Win the Week.** Determine the key numbers for each team or department and build a weekly scoreboard to measure them. Gamify Performance with simple, specific metrics.

- **Practice.** Practice to improve Performance, with roleplaying, dry runs, video recording, etc. Virtually everything can be practiced, from presentations and customer service to economic downturns and the loss of a major client.

- **Make Meetings Matter.** Meetings are our stage. Cultivate healthy drama and constructive conflict in meetings. Take them seriously by providing context and Purpose, with a set time, cadence, and reason for each. Use the 3 standard meeting types above.

CHAPTER 6

PROFIT

ENJOY THE REWARDS — AND TRACK BUSINESS HEALTH

When Bob Gardner founded Gardner Builders in 2010, the company's first office was in a psychologist's storeroom, its only sign a Post-it note with "Gardner Builders Enter Here" scrawled across the yellow sticky.

Fifteen years later, it's a $400 million company, with nearly 220 employees, three locations ("culture hubs" in Minneapolis, Milwaukee, and Duluth), and a national reputation. It ranks among the top

350 contractors in the U.S. and is licensed in 42 states, doing high-end tenant-improvement projects and major ground-up commercial construction.

The company and its Profits have grown exponentially, but not, as some might guess, by focusing on growth or Profit. Working closely with Gardner over the past decade, I've seen firsthand how its leaders truly put People first. This is a clarion call I've sounded from the first pages of this book, as I do continually with clients — *It starts with People* — but I didn't need to talk CEO Bob Gardner into the idea. It was his founding principle.

"I wanted to create a company where people would feel valued, challenged, and love to be at work," Bob says. "That was the only goal, and it remains the only goal. We could be 20 people or 2,000 people — if we lose sight of that goal, we need to stop everything and reassess."

As I've said, a great customer experience begins with a great employee experience, and leaders at Gardner have worked hard to provide one for the team. There are the obvious things — strong compensation and benefits, fantastic employee rec areas with foosball and free beer — but there's also an open atmosphere that's hard to quantify. You feel walking through the door at Gardner that this is a place where People are listened to and respected, where there are no dumb questions, and everyone is part of a team.

That environment is supported by the resources and Playbooks team members need to succeed. Gardner has Playbooks for financial, construction, and other processes, even for dealing with particular buildings where crews do repeat jobs.

"Our Playbook for IDS Center in downtown Minneapolis, for example, explains, here's how we'll walk into that building," Bob says. "We want to know how that building operates, the rules, regulations, the personalities of the people who run it and how they like to be engaged. We make sure we meet them where they are."

This sort of care reflects Gardner's Purpose — *To change the construction industry by setting the platinum standard* — and the mindset with which the company strives to achieve it. Gardner doesn't think of itself primarily as a builder, but as a hospitality company in the commercial construction business.

Bob explains it better than I can.

"What we do is based on how we treat people — our own people, our design partners and trade partners, our clients. The concept of hospitality is about how you make people feel. Service happens to you; hospitality is a dialogue, a two-way street," he says. "You tell me how you want to engage, and I'll meet you where you are and create that experience."

"Service is black-and-white, hospitality is color," Bob adds, quoting from *Unreasonable Hospitality* by Will Guidara, a book that has heavily influenced his business philosophy and team Performance. Gardner, for instance, does the kind of minor fixes for clients that many big contractors don't want to bother with — a cabinet door repair or drywall patch — and they offer "move-in day services" that put technicians on site the day a client settles into a new space, to quickly handle the stuff that typically takes months to get fixed.

I don't want to suggest that leaders at Gardner don't pay attention to Profit. Of course, they do — it just doesn't top the list.

"Profit has to be one of the things you focus on because if you don't have it, you don't have a business, so that's base funda-mentals," Bob says. "But we don't make every business decision based on how much money we'll make. If you focus on treating people well, profitability will flow, and that's been proven time and time again. If we show up differently, engage in a different way, the profit will come."

▌ INEVITABLE PROFITS

Gardner Builders could be the poster business for this chapter on our fifth and final principle, Profits. This is true not because the company's Profits have grown extraordinarily, though they have, it's because Bob Gardner and other leaders understand that if you focus on the fundamentals — People, Purpose, Playbooks, and Performance — Profits almost inevitably follow.

This is a central irony of business — if your Purpose is Profits, you're less likely to make them.

Of course, we all want to earn a Profit, but that shouldn't be your starting point, any more than carpet and window coverings are the architect's starting point. Such finishes are important, but we call them *finishes* because they come last. They are the final layer, and if you have a well-made building with a great design, it will steer you toward those appointments. Focus too heavily on colors and trim early on, to the detriment of structure, and you won't have a building to decorate. Worry about the bones, our first four principles, and the rest will come.

Profits are the reward for our labor and a pillar supporting People and culture, but they are an output, not an input. We need to worry about the People helping us to climb the mountain, our strategies for getting there, and why we're going — not the drink we'll sip or the video we'll shoot on the highest peak. That stuff will come, but if it's at the center of your journey, you're on a fool's errand.

Remember the formula I introduced early in the book, the recipe at the heart of what we do as Pinnacle Business Guides:

PEOPLE + PURPOSE + PLAYBOOKS

There's a reason Profits is the last of our five principles. If you build it, they will come. The *they* in this formulation is Profits, and the *it* is organizational health, not a baseball field (unless you happen to own a major league team). The truly great companies like Gardner Builders start with People and work their way through Purpose, process, and strategy to create Profits.

In a sense, Profits are reverse engineered, your company designed and built from the inside out, like a great building or a laptop. Apple makes beautiful products with revolutionary designs, but they all start with the operating system — that's the real key to success. You, too, need a crack operating system — whether it's Pinnacle's, another company's, or homegrown — as you build from the inside out.

BACKTRACK FROM EARNINGS, AND THEY'RE USUALLY THE RESULT OF A GREAT CUSTOMER EXPERIENCE, WHICH IS THE RESULT OF A GREAT EMPLOYEE EXPERIENCE, WHICH IS THE RESULT OF VALUING YOUR PEOPLE, INSTILLING A SENSE OF PURPOSE, AND UPPING PERFORMANCE THROUGHOUT THE ORGANIZATION. I'VE PRESENTED SOME GREAT EXAMPLES IN THESE PAGES OF PROFITABLE COMPANIES THAT ARE DESIGNED, AS I'M RECOMMENDING, FROM THE INSIDE OUT — BUSINESSES WITH BEAUTIFUL BONES.

+ PERFORMANCE = PROFITS

Recall from Chapter 1, Hempel Real Estate, which decided to establish two investment funds of $30 million. I have no doubt that this effort will be extremely Profitable, but the impetus was a desire to improve the company's capital-raising Playbook for its People, while offering a better investment vehicle for clients.

Minneapolis Oxygen, the company I described in Chapter 2, focused heavily on People as we worked to build the organization, deciding in light of its newly articulated Purpose and core values, that most of the leadership team had to be replaced. MO2's People initiatives also boosted the overall employee experience, with everything from new quarterly coaching sessions to a refurbished employee lounge. Profits at Minneapolis Oxygen have risen by a factor of six, but that wasn't the focus or primary goal.

Some of the efforts I'm describing can actually tighten Profit margins in the short term. Hiring new leaders and rehabbing the employee lounge cost money at Minneapolis Oxygen, as will establishing investment funds at Hempel. If you made decisions based solely on the bottom line, you might avoid the expense of such measures, though they can boost Profitability over the long haul.

We've all seen companies that make Profit their starting point, substituting it for Purpose and strategy, shortsighted businesses where employees don't have adequate tools, training, or resources. The company that gets the intern to answer calls when the receptionist goes to lunch — the busiest time of day — or worse, lets them go to voicemail. The company that skimps on a holiday party and bonuses or would rather live in chaos than pay People to develop Playbooks.

We want to build vision in business, to see the Pinnacle we're climbing toward and to see clearly the People and processes that will get us there. Profits should create new sightlines. They are like binoculars, an X-ray machine, and — my favorite analogy — the machine monitoring vital signs all wrapped in one.

When Profits replace Purpose, though, they do the opposite. They become the function rather than the thing that tracks it, fostering myopia instead of vision.

PROFITS AS MARKET FEEDBACK

Profits aren't the point, and yet...they are important.

It might sound like I'm contradicting myself here. I'm not, honest! I have emphasized the idea that you should focus on our other four principles partly because if you do, Profits will follow, and partly because I never have to convince leadership teams that Profits matter. Leaders often think they matter too much, but virtually no one in business is indifferent on the subject. None of us are in business to lose money.

It's Profits that allow us to survive and thrive. Without them, as Bob Gardner points out, you won't have a business for very long. If you manage to keep the lights on without Profits, maintaining culture quickly becomes impossible. From free sodas in the breakroom to the annual awards dinner to your sponsorship of volunteer day at a local food pantry, culture costs. People cost even more, as I need to tell exactly no one running a business. Payroll is the biggest expense for most companies, not to mention the costs of training, health insurance, retirement plans, and a host of related expenditures. A dearth of Profits makes it tough to put People first — the foundation for a healthy organization.

Without Profits, you can't give back to the community, and you might not weather the next downturn, whether it stems from a new competitor, a natural disaster, or an economic slump. They allow you to reinvest in technology and to hire for critical roles before the need is dire.

Profits make all this and more possible — and take care of the owner as well as the business, since we all exit someday. Whether the business gets sold or passed on to the next generation, without Profits, its value will be paltry — in some cases, no more than the value of some desks and dated equipment (Pinnacle has Certified Exit Planning Advisors who specialize in helping owners to accelerate enterprise value and to have smooth transitions when that time comes).

These are all good reasons to pay attention to our fifth and final principle. Perhaps the biggest reason to monitor Profits, though, is that Profits monitor you. In the broadest terms, they are your source of feedback from the marketplace on how valuable your products and services are. If Profits sag, it's time to reassess what you're selling and how.

Every month, I see companies performing the same work with the same resources, facing the same competition in the same economy. One makes 2 percent on the job that another makes 8 percent on, while a third earns 15 percent in Profit. Is company number three really seven times more valuable than the first one, earning 2 percent? Of course not. That business has simply figured out how to do its work with greater efficiency.

Tracking Profits intelligently, as we'll explore, can reveal your inefficiencies, highlighting what you can address to boost earnings. Maybe your competitors have Playbooks for processes you're running ad-hoc. Maybe you have the wrong People on the bus or in the wrong seats. Maybe you can close the gap simply by leveling up B-players. A small improvement in a team member's Performance might seem negligible, but if you can achieve that small improvement across the organization 30 or 80 times, depending on your payroll, it's potentially the difference between Profit and breaking even. Analyzing your actual margins and knowing your numbers (more on this soon) uncovers the trails leading to greater Profitability.

Industry benchmarks, best practices, and trade groups such as Vistage can help here. If you're in construction, getting a feel for others' labor costs, for example, or the average ratio of office staff to workers on job sites might highlight why your Profits are anemic. If you learn from peers or a trade-group study that the billable hourly shop rate for most cabinetmakers is $55 to $80, and you bill $45 an hour, it's time to raise prices. Attorneys at your small firm spend 55 percent of their time practicing law, and the average at comparable firms is 65 percent? Consider a new administrative Playbook, and if you can't afford an admin or bookkeeper, spending on fractional help might increase Profits long term. Profit is often an indicator of shortfalls in People, Playbooks, or Performance.

All industries have their numbers — the best practices and benchmarks that can help you assess your Profitability. You want to have company that's growing in enterprise value, and that means aiming to be in the top quartile of your industry in Profitability. If you aren't there yet, what benchmarks are you falling short on? Where are you spending too much or too little compared to peers? Where can you invest or eliminate inefficiencies to grow Profits?

YOUR VITAL SIGNS

In addition to supplying feedback from the marketplace, Profits offer invaluable feedback from within and about the organization. As I mentioned above, Profits are how we monitor the company's vital signs. If you think of a business as a complicated, living thing, as I do, you understand how apt the metaphor is.

The human body is an amazing living machine full of complex systems. If it's too hot, the air conditioning kicks in, and you sweat. Get cold, and it shivers to produce heat. The body tells us when to wake and when to sleep, when to mate and eat, when to relax and when to flee or fight. It is so complicated, with so many systems and functions, doctors specialize in, by some estimates, 200 areas.

And yet, when you're admitted to a hospital, nurses monitor four main vital signs that tell them most of what they need to know about how you're doing: temperature, pulse, respiration rate, and blood pressure. These four metrics measure your body's critical base functions. They are the first step in any medical exam or hospital admission and give the first clues about possible problems or conditions affecting health. We know the normal range for those vitals and the danger zones with precision — and how some of these numbers will vary depending on age, sex, body-mass index, etc.

Beyond these four vital functions, we can measure an almost infinite number of things in the body, from gamma-wave brain activity to arterial blood flow and nerve conduction.

Businesses are the same. We can focus on a handful of vital signs that tell us most of what we need to know about health, or get lost in endless, complex measures that make it tough to see the forest for the trees. There's EBITDA (Earnings Before Interest, Taxes, Depreciation, and Amortization) and ROI (Return On Investment), of course, and basic measures like gross, operating, and net profits. From there, however, many companies are tracking dozens of measures, ratios, variances, and analyses. Business intelligence technology has helped wide-ranging, creative metrics proliferate until the business dashboard that's supposed to simplify things and provide a simple snapshot can resemble a kind of Rorschach test — a mess that says more about the interpreter than the state of the organization.

Most companies I encounter are tracking so many metrics, they have trouble figuring out what they're actually doing well and what needs work. This can leave leaders feeling as out of control as those who aren't even sure what their true profit margin is — a surprisingly common phenomenon among businesses. What, out of all the possible metrics, is important? What are we really earning, and where should we focus?

Some leadership teams are only about the numbers — the disastrous Profit as Purpose model we discussed — but the other extreme is also problematic and common. Many talented visionaries who have come up with successful products or services don't have a great grasp of finance. If that's the case, they need a 2IC, or second in command, who gets Profit and metrics. The number two should have a firm grip on operations and execution, as well as the numbers, but all leaders, including the visionary, should be at least conversant in the language of business, even if they'll never speak finance like a native.

I used to do an exercise for leadership teams with a dollar bill or 100 pennies to drive home the importance of knowing your numbers and tracking Profits. Let's talk about where the money actually goes, I would say, how each dollar is spent. How much do we spend on this nice office — rent, electric, cleaning, etc.? The group would answer 14 percent, and I'd move 14 pennies from the pile to form a new one. Payroll? That one's about 32 cents on the buck, they'd say, so I would add 32 pennies to the new pile of 14. Materials, travel, equipment, administrative costs...By the time we finished, there often would be only five or six pennies remaining.

Okay, I'd say, this is it. Here is our potential Profit, but if material costs go up, they have to come from this little pile. When we have to redo work because of mistakes, pay more for healthcare, give raises, buy a new truck, up our marketing game, get Julie and Sam new laptops, it's all coming out of these five pennies. If we're going to take care of that stuff and make money, we need to create a bigger pile — five pennies ain't gonna do it.

This demo might seem obvious, even remedial, but it can be an effective visual that makes palpable the fundamentals we so often lose sight of. Leaders are sometimes reluctant to share such numbers — net Profit in particular — with the larger team.

Why?

If you don't share the numbers, team members are playing a game without a scoreboard. Business is in essence a game, an infinite one, but a game, nonetheless. As with any game, we need ways to keep score and to communicate the stakes to our teams. Telling your People, we need to "improve margins" is about as vague and useless a guide as you could provide. It's like saying, you need to lose weight or hit the gym more. How much weight — three pounds or 80? Is my goal to fit into the suit I bought last year or to avoid an imminent coronary?

Another good reason to share your numbers internally is that if you don't, the team will think Profits are much higher than they are. People hear, "We did $20 million last year" and think half or most of that was Profit. When they understand that Profits were actually $1 million and that this is our entire cushion when the price of gas goes up, when we spend 37 percent instead of the budgeted 33 percent on labor, when supply chain issues increase our costs, they become much more motivated. *Okay,* now I get why saving 5 percent on paper and getting 3 contractor bids instead of 2 is important. They now know which levers to pull and why. We all need to know our numbers, as I said in Chapter 5, both as individuals and as organizations.

PROFIT PER X

This discussion of numbers reminds me of business guru Jim Rohn, who famously would meet with team members, his neat charts and forms assembled on the table. *Okay, Greg, tell me how many deliveries you did this week*, he'd say, or how many sessions, cold calls, leads generated, packets mailed — whatever the metric. Inevitably, Greg would say, *well, listen, because of the Super Bowl...*or *since the weather was pretty bad this week...*or *I could have done more, but I had to fill in for Dave on Tuesday, and...*

Rohn would stop Greg, or any team member reporting on any job Performance, and say something like, *no, no — thanks, but I just need the number — see, your story won't fit in my box.* I like to picture Rohn at this point, innocently displaying the tiny box in question.

Everyone has a story and wants to tell it, but at some point, you have to focus on the numbers and the story *they* are telling. For any business, there is a key number we think of as "Profit Per X," a term borrowed from Jim Collins. What is the "economic denominator" that powers your company and drives profits more than any other? What's the one key ratio you should obsess over?

The steel company Nucor, for instance, figured out that its key metric was Profit per ton of finished steel. For a wealth management firm, it was fee income per advisor, and a hardwood manufacturer decided that it should obsess over Profit per board foot.

Our tool helps leaders decide on their own economic denominator and the Profit Per X that makes sense for their business.

Once a leadership team has this simple, elegant metric, it becomes the basis for all sorts of analysis focused on maximizing Profit Per X. Which of your vendors and buyers have the biggest positive effect on your Profit Per X ratio? How can you steer work toward them and avoid those that have a negative effect? Are certain product or service lines producing less Profit Per X because they're commoditized, more labor intensive, or generally less efficient to produce? Can you shrink or eliminate them, or improve efficiency to raise Profit Per X?

One of the most powerful uses for this tool is as a customer filter. Which customers produce a lower Profit Per X? Every business has finite capacity, and we find ourselves expending enormous energy and resources on low-margin clients. Can you change pricing, terms of service, or other factors to reduce the number of such customers, steering more of your limited capacity to high-margin customers? This is an effective, often simple way to increase Profit Per X and while you're at it, reduce stress and headaches, too — a nice byproduct.

I used this tool with a client whose economic denominator was Profit per employee some years ago. That was the metric that made the most sense for the business, and when I started working with them, they clocked $2,500 in Profit per employee. With around 40 team members on payroll, it wasn't a great record. We worked on our first four principles and on the kind of analysis this tool enables, and soon, we were up to $18,000 in Profit per employee. By year three, the metric was up to something like $42,000 — a much more comfortable place to be. Improvements in People and Playbooks, better processes and sharply improved efficiency, showed in this company pulse and encouraged everyone to climb higher. Trust me, it's much more fun to work at a company making $42k per employee than $2.5k.

For another client of mine, revenue per employee was the more logical ratio. That metric was in the neighborhood of $800,000 the first year the leadership team measured it. The next year it was around $750,000 per employee, and then it dipped further. This was cause for a timeout and serious analysis. The price of the product kept rising, but revenue per employee was falling — not exactly a sign of efficiency. The business was doing lots of things well, but leaders realized it was becoming too bureaucratic, political, and internally focused. The dip in this vital sign spurred an effort to streamline and cut bureaucracy, as well as a decision to freeze headcount. Leaders did not say no to new hires — People could still be moved, replaced, etc. — but the team realized that any additional headcount would simply pander to creeping inefficiency.

SCAN TO DOWNLOAD

Profit Per X can be sobering in such cases and a source of discipline. Without it or a similar vital sign, executives sometimes think they're Performing much better than they are. Basketball coach John Wooden used to say, "Don't mistake activity for achievement," words every business should live by.

Showing up, sorting emails, attending meetings, and rushing through corridors sure looks like work, but busy does not equal productive. What has actually been accomplished at the end of the day, week, month? How much has been earned per employee or per whatever item makes sense for your organization?

We might translate Wooden's wisdom into the language of finance by applying it to revenue, too: Don't mistake revenue for Profits. I have seen $2 million companies that chug along with six or seven People, making $400,000 in Profit. A few years later, they're doing $10 million in revenue and making $300,000. This is not a well-run company, and if they're not careful, they wake up one day saying, we did $20 million last year, and we lost $400,000. How quickly can you pull the fire alarm then, before the bank calls in the note or you can't make payroll or pay the credit card bill? We've all read stories of employees arriving at work Monday morning to find the doors padlocked and the boss gone. How'd that happen? They seemed healthy enough. If leaders aren't tracking the company's vital signs, they can be as surprised by its collapse as employees.

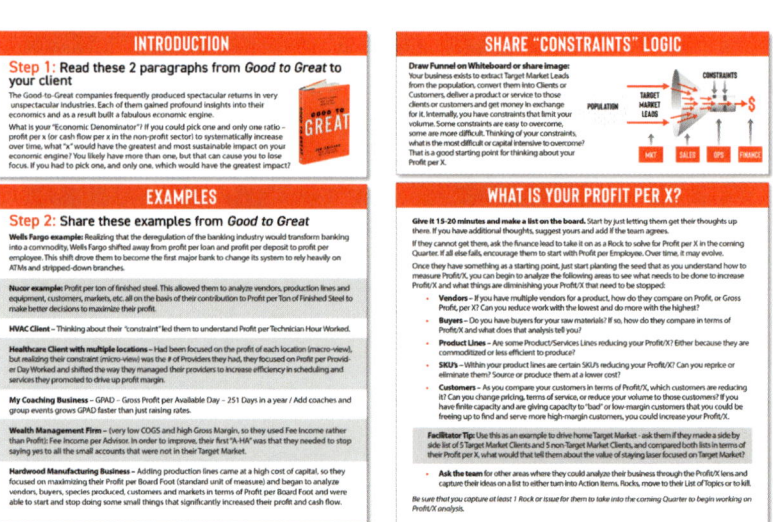

STRATEGIC VISION & EXECUTION PLAN

Knowing our numbers — figuring out the right vital signs, Profit Per X, etc. — is useless if we don't track and analyze them. How do we keep it all together, make sense of the metrics as a team, and use them to focus our efforts? How do we translate numbers into action?

For starters, any leadership team should meet monthly to discuss company finances. At Pinnacle Business Guides, we call this the Financial & Rock Accountability Meeting, a meeting format I've touched on already. This is where we gather all relevant numbers and reports to discuss, to build strategy and hold People accountable. How do our vital signs look? Is there a trend in our Profit, and what's being done to improve that ratio?

Leaders report on the quarterly financial Rocks they own at this meeting, detailing their progress and plans moving forward. If there are deviations in the general ledger, we can do a deep dive on those, but we also should save space for one or two big agenda items that either improve our financial situation or help get those financial Rocks back on track. If we've budgeted 32 percent for labor and it came in at 36 percent last month, this is the place to figure out why and how to address the issue. If our average accounts receivable days, or DSO (Days Sales Outstanding), is rising, we tackle the problem here before it spirals.

At this meeting, and every meeting, leaders should have and reference what at Pinnacle, we call The Strategic Vision & Execution Plan. This is one of our most important tools because it integrates other bedrock tools to show how we plan to grow Profits and deliver on our Purpose as we climb. The simplicity, organization, and breadth of information on this two-page map make it invaluable. I think of it as the trail map for your journey — and ours. Pinnacle's Strategic Vision & Execution

Plan is never far from my fingertips because it summarizes our vision, growth plan, and strategic goals, telling everyone on the team, *this is what matters!*

**SCAN TO
DOWNLOAD**

Purpose gets top billing in this document, in the top left corner, followed closely by our Pinnacle goal and annual growth plan summary, which lists targets for revenue and Profits, as well as key metrics. We then list our core values, mid-term milestones, and major annual goals. The bottom of the first page leaves space for key trends or other big factors affecting our business.

The second page, refreshed every 90 days at our Quarterly Summits, drills down into the quarterly execution that will move us forward on the annual goals listed on the first page. It has quarterly targets for revenue and Profits, as well as key metrics. We name a quarterly theme here to build focus, list quarterly Rocks, brand promises, KPIs, strengths, and things we say no to!

This sounds like a lot of info — in fact, it is — but it's presented clearly and logically, with pleasing graphics in a way that I think makes it an incredibly useful snapshot. But don't take my word for it.

"So often we have this anxiety around scaling, thinking about what's going to help you scale, what will hold you back," says Chris Maxson, a Pinnacle client and owner of Acucraft, a company that makes exotic custom fireplaces for clients all over the world. "Having a Guide really helped reduce that anxiety and so did having a Strategic Vision & Execution Plan. It's a map for scaling. All I need for the next year is on this two-page sheet."

Like the Profit Per X tool, our Strategic Vision & Execution Plan keeps leaders focused on the things that boost Profits, help us grow, and align with our core values and Purpose. As any business leader knows, creating this sort of focus is half the battle.

I thought about our Strategic Vision recently while teaching my daughter, Samantha, to drive. She's doing great behind the wheel, but I find myself telling her repeatedly to look up. She's focused on the next hundred feet, fixated on the road immediately in front of her rather than on the upcoming traffic light or turn. I understand that urge, but as I've explained to her, if you get your head up and look into that approaching curve, commit to it, as racecar drivers say, you'll take it more smoothly and can even accelerate a little as you exit the corner.

This, as the name implies, is what the Strategic *Vision* & Execution Plan does. It helps leaders get their heads up, see into that upcoming curve, and take it so smoothly, they're accelerating before the road straightens out. We can't know every pothole and obstacle that will appear on the road as we drive it, but like Samantha learning to train her attention on the approaching curve, our heads are up and focused on that distant spot as we steer into it, making the journey, including its sharpest turns, much smoother.

The info on our Strategic Vision & Execution Plan reminds us who we are and how we make Profits. This might sound so obvious as to be unnecessary, but even many companies with strong culture know less about their Profit drivers than they should. They look for customers, meaning anyone who will pay them, and then do "work" for those clients, meaning anything that falls within their broad purview, using the process that seems most familiar or convenient or suits their mood that day.

Such an approach is short on both vision and strategy.

For starters, not all work is created equal. Once you understand that key ratio, you can use your Strategic Vision & Execution Plan to steer the company toward the kind of work that offers higher Profit Per X and aligns with your Purpose. My longtime customer Comstock Construction, a century-old firm in Wahpeton, ND, for instance, used to do an enormous about of bid work, much of it for government projects. They realized over time that negotiated work — no bids necessary — offers much better margins. They used their Strategic Vision & Execution Plan to focus attention on those jobs, which now account for around 90 percent of their business.

Not all customers are created equal, either. As you closely monitor your vital signs and Profit, you'll realize in concrete terms that some customers come with work, more headaches, and less Profit — often because they don't match your culture. Sometimes these are one-offs, but sometimes a pattern emerges, and you realize that an entire category of customer just isn't a good fit. When you have this epiphany, use your Strategic Vision & Execution Plan to say no to this group of customers or businesses.

Certain processes, or parts of them, can also be dropped. Pro-liferating and perplexing processes kill Profits! (Forgive all those Ps.) Building Playbooks — efficient, documented, repeat-able, and scalable — and saying no to the dozens of ad-hoc processes they can replace is one of the best ways to boost Profits and add value to your company.

Many of our clients — Pinnacle Business Guides, too, for that matter — list "things to say no to" as part of their Strategic Vision & Execution Plans. This list can include certain kinds of work or customers, as we've seen, as well as vendors, tactics, types of hiring, etc. Saying no is the soul of strategy and one of the hardest things to learn as a leader. If you can't say no, you're trying to be all things to all People — in other words, you don't have a strategy. Look at the amazing companies you want to emulate, and you'll find that "addition by subtraction" — doing less and doing it better — was usually a critical part of their journeys.

THE IMPACT OF ONE

This has been perhaps our most pragmatic, numbers-heavy chapter. For that reason and because I want you to leave this book feeling that you got your money's worth, I have saved two of our most inspiring Profit tools for last. These are simple measures you can use on your own to raise your Profit margin starting tomorrow.

There are no silver bullets in business, despite the promise I just made. That's actually the point of the first tool, The Impact of One, which celebrates and harnesses incrementalism. Great athletes understand that seconds, ounces, and centimeters are the stuff of victory. Those wrestlers eating carrot sticks in the school cafeteria, the swimmers shaving every bit of body hair? They're all about the Impact of One.

SCAN TO
DOWNLOAD

This tool couldn't be simpler and is extremely effective when taught to everyone in every department. Here's how it works: Systematically ask each person in each department to think of and share one thing they could do each day to have a positive impact on the business. No item is too small and no team member exempt. Every department, every person — one thing.

The actual Pinnacle tool shares dozens of possibilities for team members in departments ranging from finance to operations, by way of example (I'll explain how to access those tools and our Guides in the conclusion). In your marketing department, for instance, People might generate one more lead per week, increase conversion rates by 1 percent, or work to get one more positive customer review per week. In operations, someone can commit to making one less mistake per day, shipping one more item per day, or reducing energy consumption by 1 percent. A team member in customer service could decide to create one more personalized customer experience or one additional "wow" moment for a client.

Is improving delivery times by 1 percent going to make a noticeable difference in your bottom line? Nope. But when that one is added to all the other ones across the whole organization — 1 + 1 + 1... x 30 or 80 or 200 — it will. The increments add up like pennies. Worry about the pence and the pounds will take care of themselves, the old saying goes. We want to worry about the pounds, er dollars, too, but part of the point of this tool and that aphorism is to change mindsets. We gamify the notion of Performance, make the improvement easily achievable, dare I say, even fun, and team members begin to internalize it. *What else can I do just a little bit better, they think, a little bit faster, with a little more attention to detail?* Those *ones* add up, and the new outlook becomes a part of your culture, boosting Profitability.

If you are sharing your numbers, as I've recommended, team members will understand against the backdrop of actual company Profits, how important these incremental improvements can be. If our Profits totaled 5 percent, or $1.2 million last year, not the $12 million everyone assumed, and they understand how many things have a claim on that cushion, turning 5 percent into 6 percent or 8 percent this year will take on some urgency. The Impact of One asks your People to come together as a team on this relatively easy climb but it also empowers each of them to individually choose, plan, and execute their one improvement. The tool stokes creativity and leadership skills, creating a sense of ownership. If as a business, you can feed team members' agency, as well as your Purpose and core values, with this sort of buy-in, you are well positioned to grow Profits and the organizational health they support.

The other tool I want to share here also relies on a shift in mindset, though Profit First is for the leadership team, not the whole organization. The actual Pinnacle tool gets slightly more analytical than the version I'll share here, but the basic idea is simple. Profits can be measured in many ways, but most leaders I encounter use this standard formula for simple Profits:

SALES − EXPENSES = PROFIT

Look familiar? Profit, of course, comes last, after expenses have been paid, often leaving very little. But in our personal lives, many of us operate another way. Of course, we want to pay all of our bills, but we take a little out of each paycheck, sometimes automatically, to put in the kids' college fund, our 401k, a savings account, or a special account earmarked for travel, entertainment, or whatever. We pay ourselves first and in so doing, guarantee that we always earn a little before the pie gets split. We always have a rainy-day fund.

The Profit First tool advises us to do the same thing with our business. The new formula is:

SALES – PROFIT = EXPENSES

Rather than chasing Profits all year, we take the same approach so many households do when they set aside that $100 or $500 or whatever at the start of each month. The bills still get paid, and you generally don't miss whatever amount was taken out. The new formula forces a new discipline, and we learn somehow to work within the established parameters.

When I present this idea to leadership teams, they're sometimes confused or skeptical for a moment. Everyone has used that first formula, which has been the standard for centuries. That's just how it's done. Oh yeah? Says who? Why? You can leave here today, I tell leaders, a more Profitable company. All you have to do is change your thinking.

Easier said than done, I know, but I usually see the lightbulbs appearing over leadership team heads pretty quickly. People generally leave inspired, deciding to become more Profitable and think in a new way.

This, in the end, is what a Pinnacle Business Guide is all about — changing the way leaders and team members think. The tools and methods are prompts, cues, ways to stoke fresh thinking and equally important, effective execution as we climb to whatever peak we've set our sights on.

MOUNTAIN LOOKBACK

- **Profits Aren't Purpose.** If your Purpose is Profits, you're less likely to make them. Start with People, followed by our next 3 principles, and Profits will come.

- **But Profits Matter.** We all want to make money. Profits keep the lights on and pay for culture. They help you give back, weather downturns, invest in technology, and hire before the need is dire.

- **Vital Signs.** Profits supply the vital signs for a living business. Figure out the Profit metrics that matter most and focus on them to track organizational health.

- **Profit Per X.** What is the "economic denominator," as Jim Collins calls it, that drives your profits? Decide on it and obsess over it. Use it to analyze customers, vendors, products, etc. Think, what changes could increase Profit Per X?

- **Strategic Vision & Execution Plan.** Keep this 2-page trail map front and center! It integrates other bedrock tools to show how we plan to grow Profits, deliver on Purpose, meet quarterly goals — and say no.

- **Impact of One.** Systematically ask each person in each department to think of and share one thing they can do each day to have a positive impact on the business

- **Profit First.** Change your formula to subtract Profits from sales, *then* pay expenses, rather than subtracting expenses first. Putting "Profits First," guarantees a rainy-day fund and forces a discipline on the organization, so expenses still get paid.

- **No Profits, No Exit.** Without Profits, your exit will simply be an assets sale, whether you're passing the business on to the next generation or selling it.

CONCLUSION

I START CLIMBING!

"People do not decide to become extraordinary," said Sir Edmund Hillary, the first mountaineer to scale to the summit of Mount Everest. "They decide to accomplish extraordinary things."

You don't have to be a genius or extraordinary, as Hillary said, to scale to your own Pinnacle. You only have to decide on a peak and commit to the climb.

People find all sorts of reasons to think small in business and plod through the foothills, without trying for their Pinnacle or even defining it. They don't have the capital, or the market conditions aren't right. They lack the resources, the right People, adequate knowledge...

So did I.

As I recounted in Chapter 1, I came from modest origins. I never had the chance to go to college, much less get an MBA, and yet, I have left some very smart competitors, even a few geniuses, in the dust. I rose to the top of whatever area I worked in. I co-founded Pinnacle Business Guides during a pandemic, and after just five years, we are on our way to our Pinnacle goal of becoming a "category-of-one" company, the brand against which every business in our space gets measured.

I don't mention this to brag — just the opposite. I have succeeded repeatedly not because I'm extraordinary but because I sighted an ambitious summit, decided to scale to it, and assembled a crack team that could help me climb there.

So can you.

What is the alternative? As I've argued repeatedly, if you're not rising as a business, you're falling (the only way to coast is downhill!) You need a Strategic Vision & Execution Plan to grow your business and add value or you will shrink and lose value. Guaranteed.

This is as true of the small retailer on the corner as it is of the behemoths traded on Wall Street. Consider this sobering fact: Most Fortune 500 companies that made the list 20 years are now off it — you read that right, *most*! Why? They couldn't adapt or innovate. They were inefficient. They kept the wrong People in key seats. They failed to face disruptions in technology and upstart competitors. In short, they did not have the kind of Strategic Vision or plan to execute it that Pinnacle Business Guides help clients build.

If Fortune 500 companies tumble down the mountain at that frequency, do you really think you're immune at whatever elevation you're camping?

You can follow those companies down the slopes or move in the opposite direction, climbing with the stamina and determination of the great companies we've explored here — the Gardner Builders, Hempel Real Estates, and Discover Strengths of the world. If the impressive climbs that these businesses have undertaken seem impossible from your vantage, recall where they started not so long ago.

CEO Josh Krsnak was the first employee of Jon Hempel when he joined Hempel Real Estate. He eventually bought the small company and two decades later, had overseen the purchase and development of more than $1 billion in commercial property. Bob Gardner started Gardner Builders, the hospitality company that does commercial construction, in 2010 with an "office" in a psychologist's storeroom and a Post-it note for a sign. Fifteen years later, it's a $400 million company with a national reputation.

Growing in this way, ascending to the highest peaks, starts with the basic decision to climb, to move in the right direction. Together, we decide on a Pinnacle and assemble a team that can move you toward that main goal. We create a Strategic Vision & Execution Plan to realize it. Growth doesn't happen overnight, but your team gets bigger and better over the next year. Processes improve. Revenue and profits increase. The margins grow more predictable, and the business gets healthier, which means its overall value rises, too.

Pinnacle has plenty of clients who have seen massive growth, but if in the near term we can lift net profit from $2M to $3M *and* reposition the company so that buyers pay closer to a 7x multiple instead of 3.5x, your valuation could jump from roughly $7M to $21M — triple the value.

This is the sort of progress we see regularly with clients, and I want to emphasize that the process doesn't involve a silver bullet. The momentum starts with the same approach that makes our Impact of One tool so effective. It's about doing things a little bit faster, making systems a little more efficient, building in more attention to detail and a sharper focus on execution. New formats for goals and meetings help. You gradually get the right People in the right seats, and everyone Performs a little better.

The improvements feed off each other, and soon, you realize, you're doing a lot of things better.

This was Discover Strength's journey as it set out to deliver on its Purpose of leading the movement of evidence-based exercise. The business was small, with three locations, $700,000 in revenue, and a dream. How could this little David go up against the Goliaths of LA Fitness, Planet Fitness, and the other multi-billion-dollar giants that dominate this space?

Discover Strength decided to accomplish something extraordinary, and, to expand on Sir Edmund Hillary's dictum, I would add that this happens by focusing intently on the ordinary, the things lesser companies consider inconsequential: How does the person at the front desk greet customers? Do you have a bulletproof Playbook for that process? How do we make sure no team member is watching a cell phone instead of clients? How do we guarantee that every exercise session ends with "a fond farewell" and the question that concludes all five-star experiences: *Is there anything else I can help you with today?*

Discover Strength's handful of 2,000-square-foot studios went head-to-head with the megaplexes of Planet Fitness and LA Fitness, with their giant pools, saunas, and spa treatments. Undaunted, Discover Strength hired A-players, built platinum Playbooks, and offered an exceptional experience. Driven by the conviction of the company's Purpose, we have figured out ways to systemize the predictable to humanize the exceptional.

As I write this, Discover Strength's CEO, Luke Carlson, was recently named Chairman of the Board for The Health & Fitness Association, a global organization representing thousands of

health and fitness clubs. He's now influencing policy interna-
tionally as a leader of his industry's premiere trade group. I can't
think of a better way to lead the movement of evidence-based
exercise — his Purpose. Now, the giant players sitting at the
table with Luke are wondering, how does this company have a
Net Promoter Score in the mid-90s? What model allows them
to turn a profit on new stores so quickly? Why do all these
topnotch physiologists with four-year degrees want to work for
them?

You, too, can rise to the top of your mountain, the brand that
competitors wish they could emulate — a Discover Strength,
Hempel Real Estate, or Gardner Builders. You can follow the
same model by building better training and Playbooks, stronger
culture, and enhanced Performance. The footprints, as I've said,
are already in the snow. Every mountain has been climbed. You
only need an expert Guide to help you uncover the best existing
trail.

That's *our* Purpose at Pinnacle, to help our clients grow and
become more valuable, to turn every business we guide into
a great place for People to work, a destination for A-players,
where team members develop while practicing their craft. As
we methodically address People, Purpose, Playbooks, and
Performance with new clients, something magical happens.
Momentum kicks in, and like a powerful flywheel, all the
small improvements accrue a cumulative, unstoppable force.
A-players begin attracting A-players. Efficient new systems
start running themselves. Morale rises and so do Profits. The
business truly starts to run like a machine, and the path that
looked too steep suddenly appears scalable.

Here are some concrete ways we can help you start on this journey:

Check out PinnacleBusinessGuides.com for more info on our methods, offerings, and the bedrock tools we've discussed here.

From our website, you can also schedule a conversation with a Guide and arrange to have one visit your company to do a workshop or presentation.

Take our free Baseline Assessment, which provides a good snapshot of organizational health and will provide your scores on each of our five principles as part of a 10-page report, at: PinnacleBusinessGuides.com/Tools/ Baseline-Assessment.

I've built on the work of many great business thinkers here and recommend that you read them in their entirety. Check out our favorites in the reading list that follows.

I will leave you with one more quote from Sir Edmund Hillary:

> ❝ *IT'S NOT THE MOUNTAIN WE CONQUER,*
> *BUT OURSELVES."*

Growth and organizational health are in your hands. It's up to you.

Decide on your Pinnacle, commit to the climb, and enjoy the view!